Leading Happiness

How the Best Leaders Put Happiness First to Create Phenomenal Business Results and a Better World

Alexander Kjerulf

Leading With Happiness: How the Best Leaders Put Happiness First to Create Phenomenal Business Results and a Better World

First published in 2017

ISBN-13: 978-87-994513-6-4

Praise for this book

“Leading with happiness is compelling—it’s useful, well-researched, and downright fun to read. I especially loved Kjerulf's insights about what “happy leadership” is and is not, and his stories and strategies about leading with happiness during tough times. Kjerulf's advice “If you have their back, they’ll have yours” are words that every leader ought to live every day."

- Robert Sutton, Stanford professor and author of The Asshole Survival Guide: How to Deal with People Who Treat You Like Dirt.

"What an inspiring book. Every leader should read it and learn how to promote happiness for employees, customers, suppliers, investors, and even the leader him- or herself. That type of leadership has been integral to our success and I know it will boost your results too."

- Garry Ridge, CEO WD-40 Company

“Alex has done it again. He has written a book that helps leaders get happier and better and, most importantly, helps their teams get better. And happier. If you follow the simple steps he lays out and adopt the worldview he suggests, I will lay a substantial wager your company will do well. Very well. Read this book. The read it again. And put the ideas into practice. You will be well served.”

- Srikumar Rao, TED speaker and author of Happiness at Work

“We all have to develop and improve as individuals and organizations. The digital revolution of the last ten years has meant that many of us are available 24/7, which is not optimal. It’s time to combine the demand for ever-increasing efficiency with happiness, so we don’t burn out. This book will show you how.”

- Søren Lockwood, CEO SEB Pension Denmark

“This book is very inspiring. Vega IT is all about happiness at work but I also love what Alexander wrote about customer happiness. I made many notes on ideas I had while reading those sections of the book and I look forward to start practicing them in the future.”

- Sasa Popovic, CEO Vega IT Sourcing

“This wonderful book gives you a blueprint for improving your business and the world. The evidence and the tools are right here in your hands. The rest is up to you!”

- Mikael Kamber, news anchor and author

“As a leader, don't I have enough on my plate? Now I have to concern myself with something as ethereal as happiness? Please Alexander Kjerulf, tell me it's not true. Oh, but it is true and it may be the grandest truth of all. And ... there is a secret waiting for you, the leader, inside this book. Happiness won't add to your workload, but decrease it, it won't add to your stresses, but lessen them. This book is not ethereal, nor is it's subject. THIS is as real as it gets!”

- Rich Sheridan CEO Menlo Innovations, Author Joy, Inc.: How We Built a Workplace People Love.

“Here at Zappos, we believe that the key to happy customers and a growing bottom line is happier employees. This book is a great read for customer-centric companies.”

- Jamie Naughton, Chief of Staff Zappos.com, inc.

Praise for Happy Hour is 9 to 5

"It's very, very good. It's incredibly well written, full of insights, and there are exercises to improve your own happiness at work. You can't ask for more than that!"

– David Maister, author of Practice What You Preach

"I have read well over 100 articles/books on topics covering happiness in the workplace and your book was by far one of the best. In fact, it was so informative that I went on and sent the link to your book to my entire professional network."

– Chris Hollins, President, talentgrade.com

"The book is witty, fun to read, and packed with useful (and practical) information. If you want to boost creativity, morale and employee engagement, this book is a must read."

- Stephen Shapiro, author of Best Practices are Stupid and 24/7 Innovation

"I have read and re-read this incredibly entertaining and easy to read book. I cannot express how important this subject is and how well this book conveys the way of creating the workplaces of the future. It is pregnant with good information that has practical ideas of how people can immediately start applying in their workplaces. It is easily the best book on this subject that I have read."

- Fraser Carey, founder of Palazzo Baths

"Alexander Kjerulf's book makes a powerful argument that a happy workplace is good business. Happy employees are more productive, more creative, healthier, and cause less problems. Best of all, this book outlines a sure-fire way to transform the workplace. I give this book my heartiest endorsement."

- Fred Gratzon, founder of Telegroup and author of The Lazy Way to Success

Contents

Introduction....2
Why Lead with Happiness?....6
Let's get philosophical....7
Happy countries....13
Happiness is the ultimate why....14
This chapter in tweets....15
The science of happiness....17
Positive psychology....18
You can raise your own and others' happiness....19
Happiness is highly emotional....20
Emotions matter—a lot!....22
Satisfaction alone is not happiness....25
Happiness can be reliably measured....26
Emotions are contagious....26
Negativity bias affects everything....28
Gratitude makes us happy....29
Small, simple actions make us happy....30
Happiness is highly social....30
Making others happy makes us happier....31
What neuroscience tells us about happiness....32
Mirror neurons....33
Social isolation/rejection causes pain....34
Healthy brains know right from wrong....34
Positive surprises make us happy....35
This chapter in tweets....36
What is happy leadership....38
What happy leadership is not....41
It's not perfect eternal happiness....41
It's not about a comfortable or easy work life....42
It's not positive thinking....43
This chapter in tweets....47
Happy leaders start with themselves....48
Get happy at work yourself....49
If you're happy and you know it....51
Move....52

Sleep..53
Practice gratitude...55
Maintain your relationships...56
Get advice...57
Stop and think...58
Don't overwork...61
This chapter in tweets..64
Happiness for employees..66
What you should know about happy employees.............67
How do leaders make employees happier?....................78
Happy employees come first.......................................103
This chapter in tweets...104
Happiness for customers...106
Make your customer awesome....................................108
Help customers track and celebrate their progress......109
Help your customers help others..................................110
Do what's right for the customer..................................111
Have fun with your customers.....................................113
Random acts of customer kindness...............................114
Let your employees be themselves................................117
Measure your employees on customer happiness.........118
Connect with customers..120
Help customers in difficult situations..........................122
The customer is not always right.................................124
This chapter in tweets...127
Make the world happy...129
Have a vision for happiness..129
Give more than just money...132
Sustainability and beyond..133
Make suppliers, vendors, and partners happy.............135
Make unions happy..137
Make investors happy..137
This chapter in tweets...141
Leading with happiness in tough times........................142
How Xilinx got through its biggest crisis......................142
If you have their backs, they'll have yours...................150
This chapter in tweets...152
The challenges of leading with happiness....................153
Business schools arc stuck in the past.........................154

Happy leaders are sometimes weeded out....................156
Unhappy leaders promote in their own image..............157
"Work sucks—everybody knows that."..........................159
No pain, no gain..160
Power does bad things to us..162
The good news...163
This chapter in tweets..164
Go forth and be happy...165

This book is dedicated to everyone brave and crazy enough to believe that we're really just here on this planet to make each other happy.

Introduction

Just think for a second what it would be like to live in a world where business leaders routinely put happiness first. Imagine the business world turned into an overall force for good, enhancing not only profits but also people's lives.

Sadly, this is not currently the case. It's long been a truism that business leadership is about maximizing results, whatever it takes. As the economist Milton Friedman depressingly put it in a very influential 1970 New York Times op-ed[1]:

The business of business is business.

He argued that CEOs who focused on anything besides enhancing shareholder value were failing in their duties and should be fired or sued. This kind of thinking is still prevalent in the business world, and it leads to incredibly damaging attitudes and actions. This kind of thinking lets leaders do things like:

- Fire thousands of employees if it will raise stock prices temporarily.
- Pollute and damage the environment to save money.
- Promote a culture of overwork that works employees to the bone, hurting their careers, their health and their personal lives.
- Confuse and cheat customers into buying as much as possible at the highest price possible, rather than helping customers buy what they want and need.
- Exploit workers financially, paying them as little as they

can get away with to make more money for their investors.

- Create toxic cultures where employees work in near-constant fear and frustration.

You may think me dystopian, but these things happen in corporations all over the world. And ultimately leaders think that they are right to do these kinds of things because their main responsibility is shareholder value. They feel no obligation to do good in the world—or even to avoid doing bad.

In fact, leaders have been so immersed in this kind of thinking that they can do incredible harm and feel no remorse. I have seen way too many press releases where a CEO announces firing thousands of employees to "enhance shareholder value" without showing the tiniest shred of regret or emotional investment in the fact that their leadership is now harming thousands of families. Other leaders are more pragmatic and apathetic, having never really taken the time to consider what impact they have or want to have through their leadership.

And that is why the world needs a new kind of leader who is motivated primarily by doing good. Or, in other words, by increasing happiness. In writing this book, I got to meet with many such leaders and learn what drives them to put happiness first and how they have used it in their leadership and I can't wait to share their stories with you.

They are not perfect people, but they have a clear vision of what they want to improve in the world, and rather than just maximizing shareholder value, they want to create more happiness in four specific domains:

1. For themselves
2. For their employees
3. For their customers
4. For the community/world

These leaders create organizations that are a force for good in the world. They lead in a way that is sustainable—not just environmentally but also economically and psychologically.

Their employees' lives are better and happier for working

there. Customers' lives are improved by the company's services or products. And the world is in some way a better place because their company exists. And don't ignore the first one: These leaders are happier themselves because they know that their leadership is making things better, not worse. Finally, happy leaders create better results for their organizations, because happiness has a long list of positive effects on the bottom line.

The title of this book should be read two ways:

1. Leading with Happiness *as the goal*—Your ultimate goal as a leader is to increase the amount of happiness in the world.
2. Leading with happiness *as a tool*—You incorporate happiness into the way you lead and make it your main leadership tool.

This reflects the dual nature of happiness—that it is both a *goal* and a *practice*.

The book is written for organizational leaders at every level in all kinds of workplaces. All leaders can lead with happiness, from CEOs to middle managers, and this type of leadership can be applied not only in business but also in charity, politics, arts, military, religion, or anywhere else humans organize to get something done.

In reading this book, you will learn:

- *What* happy leadership is, based on ancient philosophy and brand new scientific discoveries.
- *Why* happiness should be the main focus of leadership.
- *How* to lead with happiness, with inspiring examples from amazing leaders all over the world in many different types of organizations.

The first two chapters of the book lay the theoretical framework, explaining why we should even care about happiness and laying out the latest research findings from psychology and neuroscience that uncover what makes us happy. In the third chapter, we use those theories to define exactly what happy leadership is and isn't.

After that, we get practical with four chapters that go in depth with how leaders can create more happiness for themselves, their employees, their customers, and the wider community.

The next chapter is on how to lead with happiness in tough times. All teams and organizations will face a crisis sooner or later, and adversity makes focusing on happiness harder, but more important than ever.

Leading with happiness is not necessarily easy, and the next chapter lists the main challenges you may face and how to overcome them.

The final chapter is a call to action to help you get started on applying this in practice—because happiness is something we do.

Every claim in this book is supported by scientific research and the book is fully annotated with references and links to all sources, so you can look up and study the research that has inspired me. In addition to including all the references in the book itself, I have also placed a link collection on the book's website at:

www.leadingwithhappiness.com.

On this website, you can also find more resources, videos, a literature list, and download a free workbook with some more useful exercises. And most importantly, you can share your experiences and give feedback on the book. I really, really want to know what you think and how you've applied what you've read, so please go there and share any thoughts, comments, or experiences.

Happy reading!

Why Lead with Happiness?

Bob Chapman is the CEO and chairman of Barry-Wehmiller, a $3 billion global manufacturing business headquartered in St. Louis, Missouri with nearly 12,000 team members around the world. In his excellent book "Everybody Matters: The Extraordinary Power of Caring for Your People Like Family," he describes how he has created a company that focuses on the well-being of all stakeholders, not just the shareholders. This includes giving employees trust and freedom, and even going to extraordinary lengths to avoid layoffs in hard times.

This culture recently proved its value. Chapman was in France to negotiate Barry-Wehmiller's takeover of a French company. France has very strict labor laws, so this acquisition required approval from unions and the workers' council. As you can probably imagine, the French workers were very skeptical about Americans coming in and buying part of a prominent French company, and their opposition could have doomed the acquisition. But when Bob sat down with them, here's what they said: "We saw your operation in Paris. We saw the way your people were treated in Paris, and studied your culture. And we want you to buy our company."

Bob was touched, especially when the gentleman sitting next to him who was the chairman of the workers' council said, "Mr. Chapman, we've been waiting for you for thirty-two years." And the chairman began crying.

In Barry-Wehmiller, people matter. Working there should be a positive factor and make their lives better overall. But why has

Bob chosen this approach? When I interviewed him for this book, he put it very clearly:

> *Leadership is the stewardship of the lives entrusted to you.*
>
> *It starts with our fundamental responsibility for the lives of people who we have the privilege of leading.*
>
> *Everybody wants to know that who they are and what they do matters. And when you genuinely show them that you care, it profoundly affects their lives.*

Chapman believes that leading someone is a *privilege* that carries with it a *responsibility* to lead them well, and when we do that, we can profoundly affect their lives for the better.

Why the heck should we talk about *happiness* in the context of *leadership*? This is going to seem like a strange proposition to many people, so I want to clearly state the case for why happiness is not only an integral part of leading but should be the ultimate *goal* of leadership.

Happiness is cropping up almost everywhere else. Domains as different as psychology, economics, neuroscience, education, and popular culture have all had an increasing focus on happiness lately. If it crops up in so many other places, surely it may have some relevance for leadership too.

But far beyond that, there are solid philosophical and scientific reasons why good leaders should put happiness first, and we will look at them in this chapter and the next. It may get a little theoretical, but stick around—it'll be worth it. I even included a mummified corpse and accusations of orgies and depravity in ancient Greece, just to keep things interesting.

If you prefer to get more practical, feel free to skip ahead to page 48 where we start covering *how* to lead with happiness and then maybe come back and read these chapters later.

Let's get philosophical

Some of the central questions we humans must ask ourselves are these: "Which actions are right and which are wrong? What is good or evil? What makes a person a good person?" Or to put it in the context of this book: "What is good leadership? What distinguishes a good leader from a bad one? What should leaders do and what should they avoid?"

These are not easy questions, and throughout history, people have looked for the answers in many different places. Gurus, priests, prophets, holy texts, and rulers of many different kinds have offered many different views of what we should and should not do. For some reason, many of them have been especially preoccupied with what we should not do in bed with other people.

The basic idea that there is a right and wrong is embedded in all cultures, and there is broad agreement across most cultures that some things are good (e.g., charity, kindness, honesty) and some things are bad (e.g., lying, stealing, harming others).

But *why* are some actions good and others bad? Many cultures have tried to define absolute rules for right and wrong behavior, but that turns out to be surprisingly difficult. A rule like "Lying is wrong—always tell the truth," sounds sensible, but if you were a German hiding refugee Jews in your home during World War II to save them from being taken away to the concentration camps, lying about it to the Gestapo would be a very noble act. "Don't harm or kill other people" is a great general rule but also has exceptions. What if you're a cop and a heavily armed attacker is shooting at you and your partner?

The exact same problem comes up when trying to define good leadership. While doing my research for this book, I came across many attempts by experts and pundits to define good leadership based on absolute rules like "A good leader should be decisive" or "Good leaders put the customer first" or "Good leaders have confidence and charisma." While there's nothing wrong with each of these, it's clear that they can never be universal rules. For instance, it's easy to imagine that while it's often good for a leader to have confidence, there are also times when it's good to doubt your actions and decisions and be open to the possibility that you're wrong.

Given that absolute rules for right and wrong behavior (in both life and leadership) are seemingly impossible to define, what do we do? Should we simply give up and accept that we can't say anything about what good leadership is?

It turns out there is a solution to this problem in philosophy. Let me introduce you to my favorite philosopher, Epicurus, who lived in Athens around 300 BC and was one of the intellectual heirs of Aristotle. Where Aristotle held that the goal of life was to be excellent and virtuous in thought and action, Epicurus taught that the ultimate goal of life is happiness and that all the things we need to be happy in life are easy to attain. For example, he cited friendship as a main source of happiness[2], writing:

> *Of all the means which wisdom acquires to ensure happiness throughout the whole of life, by far the most important is friendship. Friendship dances around the world, bidding us all to awaken to the recognition of happiness.*

Epicurus certainly did not ignore the value of a strong character, and absolutely recognized that virtue was important. But where Aristotle made virtue and excellence the end goal of his ethics, Epicurus saw happiness as the end goal and virtue as a path to that goal[3], writing:

> *It is impossible to live a pleasant life without living wisely and honorably and justly, and it is impossible to live wisely and honorably and justly without living pleasantly. Whenever any one of these is lacking, when, for instance, the man is not able to live wisely, though he lives honorably and justly, it is impossible for him to live a pleasant life.*

On a side note, Epicurus also famously argued that we should not fear death because fearing death just reduces your enjoyment of life. You shouldn't fear death, he argued, because once you're dead, you won't be around for it[4], saying:

> *Accustom yourself to believe that death is nothing to us, for good and evil imply awareness, and death is the privation of all awareness; therefore a right understanding that death is nothing to us makes the mortality of life enjoyable, not by adding to life an unlimited time, but by taking away the yearning after immortality.*

In ancient Greece, where people lived in fear of the capricious Greek gods and the punishments they could visit upon you in this life or in the afterlife, this in itself was a revolutionary idea.

But the central, crucial insight of Epicurus is to put *human experience* at the center of ethics and define things as good and right when they lead to more happiness in life and as wrong and evil when they lead to more pain.

Epicurus was way ahead of his time in many ways. He set up his own school in Athens called "The Garden," where he taught philosophy to anyone, even women and slaves, which was completely unheard of in a time where philosophy was for only for free men. Many Athenians were sure that he was just using them for orgies and debauchery. Why else would anyone invite women and slaves into a school? There was just no way he could be actually teaching them philosophy![5]

Ever since, Epicurus has wrongly been accused of being a mindless slave to pleasure, when his teachings say nothing of the kind. Today, we use the word Epicurean to mean "a person devoted to sensual enjoyment, especially that derived from fine food and drink." It's all terribly unfair to Epicurus, and perhaps a very early indication of the kinds of criticism people still face, when they talk about the importance of happiness.

The next big development in the philosophy of happiness came with *utilitarianism*. Here's the formal definition:

> *Utilitarianism is the doctrine that an action is right in so far as it promotes happiness, and that the greatest happiness of the greatest number should be the guiding principle of conduct.*

It is most closely associated with Jeremy Bentham, an English philosopher, jurist, and social reformer in the 18th and 19th century and it's immediately obvious that it has been inspired by Epicurus.

Let me just give a quick note on the name 'utilitarianism,' which has always confused the heck out of me, because it sounds like *utilitarian*, meaning "designed to be useful or practical rather than attractive." While Bentham defined happiness as the main goal of human life, he used a more formal term for it that he borrowed from fellow philosopher David Hume, namely *utility*:

> *By the principle of* utility *is meant that principle which approves or disapproves of every action whatsoever, according to the tendency which it appears to have to augment or diminish the happiness of the party whose interest is in question: or, what is the same thing in other words, to promote or to oppose that happiness.*

That's why it's called *utilitarianism*. Where Epicurus focused mostly on how individuals should lead their lives, Bentham wanted to use the same principles of happiness to drive societal reforms, which, let's face it, were badly needed in 19th century Britain. This makes him the first person to define what is good or bad in a society based on what increases the happiness or decreases the unhappiness of its people.

Bentham further argued that we should not limit these considerations to humans—we should also consider animal welfare, writing:

> *The question is not, Can they reason? nor, Can they talk? but, Can they suffer? Why should the law refuse its protection to any sensitive being?*

Animals may not be as intelligent as humans, but they have the capacity for suffering, and therefore we should treat them well too.

Interestingly, though Bentham died in 1832, you can still see him if you take a trip to London. In his will, he stipulated that his body be dissected for science and his skeleton and head be preserved in a wooden cabinet. The skeleton was padded out with hay and dressed in his clothes.

University College in London bought the whole thing in 1850 and keep it on display in their main building. For the 100th and 150th anniversaries of the college, it was brought to the meeting of the College Council, where it was listed as "present but not voting."

Let me lay one final philosopher on you. Unless you're Danish, you have probably never heard of K.E. Løgstrup. But his work has been highly influential in Scandinavia. His most famous idea was presented in the 1956 book "The Ethical Demand."[6] Here's the basic concept:

> *By our very attitude to another we help to shape that person's world. By our attitude to the other person we help to determine the scope and hue of his or her world; we make it large or small, bright or drab, rich or dull, threatening or secure. We help to shape his or her world not by theories and views but by our very attitude towards him or her.*
>
> *Herein lies the unarticulated and one might say anonymous demand that we take care of the life which trust has placed in our hands.*

To paraphrase, Løgstrup says that you never interact with another human being without holding a little bit of that person's life in your hand and that you have an ethical responsibility for how you affect that person. In other words, it is our duty to treat those around us in a way that increases their happiness.

This applies in every aspect of life, but in the workplace, we can fall into a pattern of thinking that puts other concerns first. Our attitudes towards other human beings can be negatively affected by time pressure, economic pressure, performance pressure, and so on. We know that people very quickly adopt the norms and behaviors of those around them (in social psychology calls this is called *conformity*[7]) and toxic leadership or cultures rapidly make people act in ways that border on sociopathic behavior[8]. But it doesn't matter what types of pressure your job puts on you; Løgstrup argues that none of that gives you the license to treat other people with less than the utmost respect and care. Indeed, we have an ethical demand to treat employees, customers, coworkers, vendors, and the like well. This goes double for leaders, whose behavior —good or bad—is always seen by employees and quickly adopted as the new norm. The classic Milgram Experiment is one of the scariest examples and demonstrates how easily an authority figure can get people to deliver what they believe are fatal electrical shocks to another person[9].

As we will see in the next chapter, there is also significant business advantage in happiness. Research has shown that happy leaders are more successful, happy employees are more motivated and productive, and happy companies make more money, just to mention a few of the many benefits. This means that leading with happiness is not about sacrificing business results so people can feel good. It is quite the opposite, in fact; happy leaders create much better results over time.

But I want to make this perfectly clear: Even if there wasn't the tiniest shred of evidence that happiness enhances business results, leading with happiness would still be the right thing to do ethically, simply because of the amazingly positive effects good leadership has on employees, customers and the wider world.

Happy countries

So the idea that the ultimate yardstick for good or evil, right or wrong is happiness has been with us for thousands of years and is gaining influence, even in politics. In February 2017, I was invited as a happiness expert to the World Government Summit in Dubai, an annual event focused on "the future of government" that attracts 4,000 delegates from all over the world.

Somewhat surprisingly, the main theme running through the entire event was not governing or politics or bureaucracy; it was *happiness*, specifically how government policies can further the happiness of citizens. This is the most recent frontier of happiness: How to run a country based not just on economic growth but rather on the happiness of its citizens.And the two are not as related as you might think. It is entirely possible to create economic growth in a way that does not make people any happier. For instance, GDP per capita more than doubled in the UK from 1973 to 2002, while life satisfaction stayed constant.

So the idea that happiness matters is increasingly gaining traction. Whether you're leading a team, a business, an orchestra, a charity, or a country, the main goal of your leadership should be to increase happiness for as many people as possible. If your leadership does not do that, you're doing it wrong.

Happiness is the ultimate why

> *I believe that the very purpose of our life is to seek happiness. That is clear. Whether one believes in religion or not, whether one believes in this religion or that religion, we all are seeking something better in life. So I think the very motion of our life is towards happiness.*
>
> *–The Dalai Lama*

These are the three main philosophical arguments that I have presented in this chapter:

- Epicurus: Human happiness is what defines right and wrong, good and evil. We all seek happiness, and all the things we need in life to be happy are easy to attain.
- Bentham: We should seek to maximize happiness for as many as possible—indeed for all creatures capable of feeling pleasure and pain. Good actions are those that increase the total amount of happiness in the world.
- Løgstrup: You affect every single person you interact with, and you have a responsibility to take good care of them and try to affect them positively.

Thus, happiness plays the role of the ultimate *why*. Why should we be kind to our fellow humans? Because it makes them happy. Why should we be concerned with animal welfare? Because animals can suffer or be happy too and making them suffer is wrong. Why should we fight global warming? Because the environmental devastation climate change is likely to cause will lead to untold suffering and unhappiness. Why should we give to charity? Because it increases the happiness and/or decreases the suffering of whomever the charity helps. Why is it better to live in a democracy than a dictatorship? Because people are happier when they are free. Why do we work to fight racism, sexism, and discrimination? Because biased treatments of some groups make people unhappy. Why should we work to increase the health of a population? Because being unhealthy or sick makes people unhappy.

Or to frame it in the context of leadership: Why should companies not pollute? Because polluting the environment causes suffering to animals and humans. Why should leaders treat their employees well? Because that makes employees happy. Why should we have fair salaries in general and equal pay between sexes in particular? Because unfair treatment makes people unhappy.

We can even apply this to answer the ultimate question "Why are we here? What is the meaning of life?" The answer is "We are here to be happy and make each other happy," and happiness defines what is meaningful. If you look at anything that is meaningful to you in life, I bet that at the core of it, it is about increasing happiness (or decreasing unhappiness) for you or someone else. If it isn't, is it truly meaningful?

And great workplaces recognize this. IKEA's company vision is simply this[10]:

> *At IKEA our vision is to create a better everyday life for the many people.*

This is clearly about increasing happiness for as many people as possible.

Happiness (for humans and other conscious creatures) is the ultimate yardstick for right and wrong, good and evil. The main challenge has always been to define what makes us happy or unhappy. For the longest time, we had no objective data or satisfying answers to this question. Your guess would have been as good as mine or that of a Stone Age tribe's medicine man.

But this has all changed. For the first time in human history, we have actual scientific research on what makes people happy or unhappy, and we're going to look at that in the next chapter.

This chapter in tweets

- Leaders affect every single person they lead and have a responsibility to take good care of them and treat them well.
- Happiness is cropping up almost everywhere -

psychology, economics, neuroscience, and education. Surely it's relevant in leadership too.

- Danish philosopher Løgstrup: you have an ethical responsibility to treat those around you in a way that increases their happiness.
- Even if there was no evidence that happy employees boost profits, it would still be the right thing because of the positive effects on them.
- Leaders should learn from the Greek philosopher Epicurus: we all seek happiness and all the things we need to be happy are easy to attain.
- There are no absolute rules for what good leadership is. We know it by the effect it has. Good leadership increases happiness.
- Happiness is the ultimate why. Everything we do, we do because we think it will create more happiness.
- The main goal of leadership should be to increase happiness in the world. If your leadership does not do that, you're doing it wrong.
- Leaders by definition have a large effect on others and therefore face an even larger obligation to affect them positively.

The science of happiness

It's an essential part of my job to make my orchestra happy. And I don't mean just happy "Ha ha," cheerful, having a good time, but really happy in the music, because music has a way of flowing and lifting us and our spirits and our feelings.

So my prescription is, a happy musician will be a great musician if their power is released. So the power is in them, it's not in me. If I can enable them to feel that energy, feel that power, feel the flow of the music, go on the wave of the music, then the music will work. If they're dejected or suppressed or in some way depressed, I can absolutely be certain the music won't work. So happiness is a necessity, it's not just something nice. It's an absolute necessity.

–Benjamin Zander

Benjamin Zander is a British conductor and the musical director of the Boston Philharmonic Orchestra and the Boston Philharmonic Youth Orchestra. When I met him at his home in Boston, he was 73 years old and struck me as one of the happiest and most energetic people I've ever met.

Where some conductors are notorious for being temperamental dictators who rule with an iron fist, Ben has a very different philosophy. He pointed out that no matter how good a conductor he is and how vigorously he waves his arms around, he never makes a single sound. He is completely dependent on the orchestra, and while he may be the leader, they make the music, and he discovered that happy musicians play better music. Therefore, keeping his musicians happy became a central part of his leadership.

As we saw in the last chapter, *happiness matters*. In fact, if you ask some of the big questions like "Why are we here?" or "What is the meaning of life?" the answer is quite simply that we are here to be happy and make each other happy. And given that leaders by definition have a large influence on other people, and therefore a large potential for creating happiness or unhappiness, it's especially important for leaders to put happiness first.

Given all that, we have to answer some very simple questions: What exactly is happiness and what makes people happy or unhappy? If we don't have solid answers for these questions, there is no way for us to reliably increase happiness.

Fortunately, we now have actual scientific answers, coming from two fascinating fields: Positive psychology and neuroscience. This chapter will give you an overview of the most important and fascinating findings from these two fields that are relevant for leaders.

Positive psychology

Traditional psychology looks at everything that can go wrong with our minds—psychosis, neurosis, phobia, depression, and so on—and asks how these conditions can be treated or cured. It's an incredibly important field that has had tremendous success in easing human suffering.

But in the last few decades, some psychologists have started asking the opposite question: When are we happy? What does it take for people to live good lives and thrive psychologically and physically? This field is called *Positive Psychology*[11] and has led to many important and surprising discoveries about happiness.

What I especially appreciate about positive psychology is that it is entirely evidence-based. This is not feel-good fluffy guesswork; this is hard research conducted by many research teams all over the world to figure out what the good life is. Here are some of the most important findings from positive psychology that all leaders should know.

You can raise your own and others' happiness

Let's start with the most important question: Can people affect their own happiness at all? Or is a person's happiness pre-determined and unchangeable? If the latter were the case, we might as well give up now, right?

Some of the most fascinating research on this question comes from the Minnesota Twin Family Study which compared happiness levels between identical and fraternal twins. They found that identical twins (who are genetically identical) tend to be closer to each other in happiness levels than fraternal twins (who share only as much DNA as regular siblings)[12]. This made them conclude that:

> *Nearly half of happiness can be accounted for by genetic factors. The other half is determined by life's everyday ups and downs.*
>
> *In other words, everyone is born with a certain "set point" for happiness in the same way that your household thermostat is set to maintain a certain temperature in your home. Tragedies and pleasures might affect your level of happiness. But eventually, you will return to your genetic set point, just as the temperature of your home will return to your thermostat's set point after you have let in cold air by opening a door or window.*

So, while some people are genetically pre-disposed to happiness and others are not, it's important to remember that genetics isn't destiny and the research clearly shows that there are ways to increase happiness. You can increase happiness in the short-term, i.e., in ways that make you feel better here and now but the research also shows that there is a cumulative effect so that you can also raise your long-term happiness (your set point) through a concerted effort over time[13].

Happiness is highly emotional

There are many ways to define happiness, and none of them may be perfectly right. The definition that we will use for this book is widely accepted among happiness researchers and has the additional advantage of being very simple:

> *Happiness is the frequent experience of positive emotions combined with an overall sense that life is good and meaningful.*

This definition combines two different aspects of happiness, namely:

1. Your overall emotional state, i.e., whether you spend most of your time experiencing positive or negative emotions
2. An overall satisfaction with your life circumstances

Of these two, emotions are by far the most important and also the most overlooked. We all have emotions. Some of them are positive; some are negative. Positive and negative in this context does not imply that emotions are right or wrong, it just means that some emotions feel good while others feel bad.

A happy person often experiences positive emotions and rarely (but not never) experiences negative emotions. Conversely, an unhappy person spends much of their time experiencing negative emotions[14].

Common positive emotions	**Common negative emotions**
Joy, serenity, hope, gratitude, amusement, interest, pride, awe, love, inspiration.	Loneliness, disgust, indifference, anger, sorrow, fear, frustration, sadness, embarrassment, envy.

Since happiness is so dependent on a person's emotional state, it's important to recognize that emotions change constantly and that no one can (or even should) experience positive emotions all the time. If you were to draw a simplified emotional map of someone's day, it might look something like this:

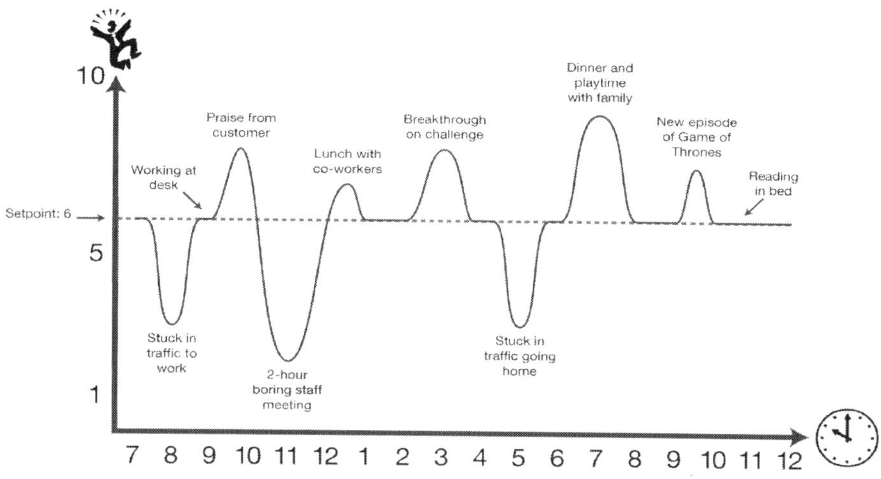

You can see how this person's emotional state varies between 0 (completely unhappy) and 10 (completely happy) depending on what is going on throughout the day. In real life, a person's emotional state would change much more often during a day, so this graph is a highly simplified view.

In this example, the person's set-point is at 6, so when nothing else is going on, that person is mildly content, which is true for most people. Also, how much emotions fluctuate depends on the person—some people have very stable emotions that only go up and down a little, others are much more emotional, experiencing deeper troughs and higher peaks.

The aim is not for people to lead a life where they are at 9 or 10 on the happiness scale all the time, the aim is to create as much happiness as possible for as many as possible. Logically, this means that there are four basic ways to increase the total amount of happiness in a person's life:

1. By living longer. The longer a person lives, the more total happiness they can experience.
2. By creating more or higher peaks of positive emotions.
3. By creating fewer or more shallow troughs of negative emotions.

4. By raising the set-point—how happy a person feels in the absence of specific stimuli

The first one (lifespan) is somewhat harder to address directly but is actually likely to follow from increasing the amount of happiness a person experiences. As we will see on page 22, a person's emotional state affects their health, and happy people live longer.

The other three are more directly under our control. In the example above, this person might eliminate some unhappiness by leaving for work earlier, so she doesn't get stuck in rush hour traffic, or by skipping the boring weekly 2-hour department meeting. She could also work to increase her set-point from 6 to 7. All of this would serve to maximize positive emotions over time, i.e., her long-term happiness.

The crucial insight here is that while emotions vary throughout our lives and it may not matter much how we feel this very second, our emotional state over time has a huge effect. Let's see what science says on that.

Emotions matter—a lot!

It's clear that emotions are fleeting and can change rapidly, but that doesn't mean that we can ignore them. People's emotional state over time turns out to have huge effects in many areas. First of all, and maybe most obviously, studies show that positive emotions have significant cognitive benefits. Happy people:

- Are more creative.
- Are faster learners.
- Are more resilient in the face of setbacks and challenges.
- Make better decisions.

Essentially, we now know that when you experience positive emotions, your mind functions in a broader and more open way. This is what Barbara Fredrickson, one of the leading researchers in positive psychology, calls the broaden-and-build effect[15]:

The broaden-and-build theory of positive emotions

suggests that positive emotions broaden one's awareness and encourage novel, varied, and exploratory thoughts and actions. Over time, this broadened behavioral repertoire builds skills and resources.

This is also confirmed by the research performed by Teresa Amabile and Steven Kramer[16] who found that:

If people are in a good mood on a given day, they're more likely to have creative ideas that day, as well as the next day, even if we take into account their mood that next day.

There seems to be a cognitive process that gets set up when people are feeling good that leads to more flexible, fluent, and original thinking, and there's actually a carryover, an incubation effect, to the next day.

Negative emotions tend to have the opposite effect, narrowing our focus, lessening our ability to think in new ways and to learn. The main cognitive advantage of mild negative emotions seems to be a slight increase in our ability to focus on routine tasks.

A person's emotional state over time also affects their mental and physical health[17]. Happy people experience:

- Less stress
- Fewer depressions
- Lower rates of cardiac disease
- Fewer strokes

As a consequence, happy people live longer. For instance, a study of aging Danish twin pairs found that the happier twin tends to live longer than the less happy one[18].

Finally, happy people are more successful in life and at work. One fascinating paper looked specifically at the impact of our emotional state over time[19]:

Our focus in this article is on happy individuals – that is, those who experience frequent positive emotions, such as joy, interest, and pride, and infrequent (though not absent) negative emotions, such as sadness, anxiety, and anger.

Using this definition, they found that:

Happy people appear to be more successful than their less-happy peers in three primary life domains: work, relationships, and health.

The results reveal that happiness is associated with and precedes numerous successful outcomes, as well as behaviors paralleling success.

Furthermore, the evidence suggests that positive emotions—the hallmark of well-being—may be the cause of many of the desirable characteristics, resources, and successes correlated with happiness.

Some people argue that emotions don't belong in the workplace; we should leave them at home and come to work and be calm, cool, and professional. In light of the research I've mentioned above, this attitude makes no sense at all. Emotions are integral to who we are; they're coming with us everywhere we go, whether we want it or not and have significant effects on our performance and wellbeing.

Why do emotions matter as much as they do? The best theory is that emotions evolved as a learning tool. Things that are good for us cause positive emotions, and we tend to seek out those things again in the future. Conversely, anything that might be a threat causes negative emotions, and we tend to avoid those going forward. So, our emotions are the most basic indicator we have of what is good or bad for us. Of course, it's not a perfect system. Drinking that fourth glass of wine on a night out with friends may feel great at the time but carry a cost the morning after.

Also, it appears that our current emotional state serves as an indicator of whether we can relax or need to be on guard. When we're in a negative emotional state, our bodies tend to be more tense and our minds more narrowly focused on anything negative around that may represent a threat. On the other hand, when we experience positive emotions, our minds are more open to new thoughts and experiences, and our bodies are more relaxed. So, while emotions are not a perfect indicator of how we're doing and what's good or bad for us, it's still the most fundamental gauge we have.

Satisfaction alone is not happiness

While satisfaction is part of happiness, many people treat the two as identical concepts. This is a mistake. For instance, many leaders ignore emotions at work and instead focus solely on *employee satisfaction*, many companies measure *customer satisfaction* instead of customer happiness, and many countries look solely at the *life satisfaction* of their citizens instead of at their emotions.

And while the two terms are definitely related, they're still different. For instance, job satisfaction is what you *think* about your job. When you sit down and weigh all the pros and cons, how satisfied are you with your work situation? This is very much a rational, intellectual, thought-based process that takes place only when you make a conscious effort to think about these things, e.g., once a year when you complete a staff satisfaction survey.

Satisfaction	**Happiness**
More rational	More emotional
Takes effort and focus	Happens automatically
After the fact	In the moment
Rare	Frequent
Few beneficial effects	Many beneficial effects

As we saw previously, happiness is much more about emotions over time, i.e., how you *feel*. On a typical day, do you experience mostly positive or mostly negative emotions? This is automatic and takes place all the time and hence tends to affect us much more deeply than satisfaction, which only matters when we are consciously making an effort to think about it.

In other words, satisfaction is how happy you are while you think about how happy you are (which is probably rarely). Your emotions govern how happy you are the rest of the time while you're actually going about your life, which is hopefully the vast majority of the time. That alone makes emotions much more relevant than satisfaction.

As we just saw, our emotional state over time has a huge effect on our well-being and performance—satisfaction, on the other hand, turns out to have much fewer beneficial effects. For instance, there is a weak correlation between job satisfaction and employee performance but a much stronger correlation between a positive emotional state and job performance[20].

Also, there is no way you can energize or excite yourself or others using the theme of satisfaction. "Come on, everybody, let's be satisfied!" is not exactly the rallying cry of the century.

Seriously, do you want to spend your life simply being satisfied? When you look back on your life, do you want to be able to say, "Well, I was perfectly satisfied"? No! Make happiness your goal. As in, "I will lead in a way that makes this a workplace where people love to work and which spreads happiness to our customers and community." It has much more potential to engage others and sends a much clearer and more inspiring message.

Happiness can be reliably measured

One objection I often hear is that happiness is such a fluffy concept that it can't be measured. So, let me just say that research clearly shows that there are reliable, valid ways to measure people's happiness using surveys that have undergone rigorous statistical and methodological verification[21].

Emotions are contagious

A participant at one of my speeches shared this story:

I had a manager once, who clearly loved his job. He was seemingly always in a good mood, had a smile on his face and was always ready to share a joke or a laugh. Even if you came to him with bad news (maybe you were going to miss a deadline), he'd listen calmly and help you figure out a plan B.

His mood spread to the entire team who loved working there and would go through fire for him.

Emotions are contagious and tend to affect those around them. Happy people lift the mood of everyone around them and unhappy people bring everyone else down.

In one fascinating experiment[22], a group of test subjects were tasked with taking part in a meeting where they acted as managers on a salary committee that negotiated the allocation of a limited sum of bonus money to their employees. Each participant played the role of a department head representing a candidate from his or her own department who had been put forth for a merit bonus increase and was trying to get as much money for that candidate as possible.

The test subjects thought they'd been assigned to present their case in a random order, but in reality, the first person to speak was an acting student who was secretly a confederate of the experimenter. These types of experiments are often quite devious, because revealing the true nature of the experiment would make it impossible to obtain any valid results. The actual content of the confederate's presentation was always the same, but his mood would be either very pleasant with frequent smiles or very unpleasant and negative. The experiment found that when the confederate displayed happiness, the other participants became happier and the group worked better together for the rest of the meeting. Think about this and make sure to always start your meetings on a positive note in the future.

Research also shows that the more attention a person gets, the more that person infects others with their mood. Since leaders, by definition, receive much more attention, this means that their emotions are the most contagious. In other words, you can make people around you happier, simply by being happy yourself and letting it show.

Negativity bias affects everything

Our minds focus more on anything that's bad than on the good. One fairly depressing review article entitled "Bad is stronger than good" sums it up like this[23]:

> *Bad emotions, bad parents, and bad feedback have more impact than good ones, and bad information is processed more thoroughly than good. Bad impressions and bad stereotypes are quicker to form and more resistant to disconfirmation than good ones.*
>
> *Hardly any exceptions (indicating greater power of good) can be found. Taken together, these findings suggest that bad is stronger than good, as a general principle across a broad range of psychological phenomena.*

Why do we have this negativity bias and why is it so pervasive? The best guess comes from evolutionary psychology. Imagine two young cavemen walking through a field on a beautiful sunny day. To their right is a dense bush, and suddenly they hear the rustling of what sounds like a big animal in that bush.

One of the cavemen has a strong negativity bias. He immediately thinks "I bet it's a sabertooth tiger that wants to eat me," and runs away as fast as he can. The other caveman is a much more positive and optimistic soul who instead thinks "What an interesting sound, I bet it's something fun and interesting. I should go check it out." He gets eaten by the sabertooth tiger and never gets to pass on his overly positive genes to the next generation unlike his more negative friend who gets to live and have kids.

While this negative focus was great for our survival in more dangerous times, it is still with us now and still affects every aspect of our thinking. This is worth watching out for, because when we overfocus on the negative, which we do, everything ends up looking worse than it is. Many workplaces are plagued by negativity bias and somehow manage to only focus on and talk about failed projects, late deadlines, dissatisfied customers, or missed goals while anything that is successful or good is ignored or taken for granted. Or as one researcher put it[24]:

> *The brain is like Velcro for negative experiences but Teflon for positive experiences.*

The good news is that we can train ourselves to focus more on the positive, for instance, by practicing gratitude.

Gratitude makes us happy

> A group of volunteers were asked to write down a few sentences about their week for 10 weeks.
>
> Some participants wrote about things they were grateful for that week, some were told to write about irritations or things that had displeased them, and some just wrote about events that had affected them (with no emphasis on them being positive or negative).
>
> After 10 weeks, those who wrote about gratitude were more optimistic and felt better about their lives. They also exercised more and had fewer visits to physicians than those who focused on sources of aggravation[25].

If you want to be happier, there are two fundamental ways you can go about it:

1. You can try to attain more of the things that make you happy; or
2. You can practice feeling grateful for the things you already have that make you happy.

Both of these are valid approaches, but studies have found that the second turns out to be particularly powerful. To begin with, it's easier. You don't need to achieve any new goals or get anything else—you just need to appreciate what you already have.

But more than that, if you're never grateful for what you have, it doesn't matter how much you have, it will never make you happy. This explains why some people seem to have everything but are still not happy—they're focused on getting more instead of feeling grateful for what they have.

Epicurus (my favorite philosopher from back in chapter 1) pointed out the same thing, saying:

> *He who forgets the good things he had yesterday becomes an old man today.*

Small, simple actions make us happy

It's tempting to think that happiness is a distant goal that requires huge changes in a person's life. The way to happiness could be through wealth, fame, perfectly healthy living, spiritual enlightenment, or something similarly complicated and difficult.

But according to research, it's a lot simpler and many small actions have been shown to have significant effects on our happiness. Berkeley University has launched a program called Greater Good in Action[26] which collects hundreds of simple, proven interventions like:

- Write a gratitude letter to a person who means a lot to you
- Perform a random act of kindness
- Keep a gratitude journal
- Make an apology
- Write a self-compassion letter

Happiness is a lot less complicated than many people think, and there are many simple actions we can take to make ourselves and others happier.

Happiness is highly social

The *Grant Study* is one of the most fascinating studies of human happiness and flourishing. It started in 1938 and has followed 268 Harvard undergraduate men for 75 years, regularly measuring them on a wide range of psychological and physical traits like personality type, IQ, drinking habits, family relationships and (my personal favorite) "hanging length of his scrotum"[27].

The current lead researcher, George Vaillant, summed up the

study like this:

> *The seventy-five years and twenty million dollars expended on the Grant Study points to a straightforward five-word conclusion: "Happiness is love. Full stop."*

Those men who had good social relationships with their spouses, parents, children, families, and friends were happier, healthier, and lived longer. They were also more successful at work and made more money. Surprisingly, it turned out that IQ had very little effect on their incomes whereas relationships mattered a lot[28]:

> *The men who scored highest on measurements of "warm relationships" earned an average of $141,000 a year more at their peak salaries (usually between ages 55 and 60).*

One of the biggest mistakes we can make about happiness is to see it as an individual pursuit, something that each of us must create for ourselves alone. I think Lily Tomlin said it best:

> *The trouble with the rat race is, that even if you win, you're still a rat.*

Humans are an inherently social species and our happiness depends hugely on the happiness of those around us. Study after study has found that we are much happier when we have rich, positive social connections to spouses/partners, family, friends, coworkers, and so on.

Making others happy makes us happier

Fred Gratzon, a successful US business leader, defines success like this:

> *Here is how I know someone is successful—If you are able to give from your abundance.*

My absolute favorite finding from positive psychology and one that has been confirmed in countless studies is that we actually derive more happiness from doing nice things for others than for ourselves. It's simply part of our nature to be altruistic, generous, and compassionate. We want to be happy and we want those around us to be happy too.

Many people have a negative view of human nature. They think that we are born selfish and bad and must be trained to behave. Only the threat of punishment, either in this life or the afterlife, is what keeps us on the straight and narrow path. But that's just not true—we are not born bad. Quite the opposite, say scientists:

> *Human children begin to behave prosocially very early in life, before two years of age. Studies have documented one-year-olds' abilities to comfort others in distress, participate in household tasks, and help adults by bringing or pointing to out-of-reach objects.*

In my favorite study on this, German researchers looked at helping behavior in toddlers[29]. A toddler saw an adult with a heavy box in his hands who needed help with some simple task, i.e., getting a cupboard open. In the videos from the experiment, you will see these small children consistently walk over and open the cupboard for the adult with no prompting from anyone. What's more, they seem to really enjoy the opportunity to help someone else. It's a very positive and devastatingly cute sight[30] and it clearly shows that wanting to make others happy with no expectation of reward is part of our nature.

What neuroscience tells us about happiness

On the very cutting edge of the happiness research, neuroscientists all over the world are studying the brain to find how pleasure and pain are expressed in terms of our actual grey matter. The better we understand our brains, the more effectively we can increase happiness[31]:

> *Psychologists have made substantial progress in mapping happiness' empirical features, and neuroscientists have made comparable progress in investigating the functional neuroanatomy of pleasure, which contributes importantly to happiness and is central to our sense of well-being.*

New technologies like MRI scanners (those big, white, noisy machines you slide people into on a tray like sliding a pizza into the oven) let scientists examine how blood flow in the brain changes depending on what the subjects are doing, thinking, or feeling, and while much of this research is in very early stages and subject to a lot of speculation, there have been some fascinating results already, which, interestingly, tend to support the findings from positive psychology. Here are some of the most fascinating and relevant findings from neuroscience that we can use to inform happy leadership.

Mirror neurons

Many important scientific discoveries are made by accident, and the story of how mirror neurons were found is a great example:

> Three Italian scientists placed electrodes in the brain of macaque monkeys to study the neurons that control the actions of its hands, for example when it picks up an item. During each experiment, they recorded the activities of a single neuron in the monkey's brain while the monkey was allowed to reach for pieces of food so the researchers could measure the neuron's response to certain movements.
>
> One scientist explains: "I think it was Fogassi, standing next to a bowl of fruit and reaching for a banana when some of the monkey's neurons reacted. How could this happen, when the monkey did not move? At first, we thought it was a flaw in our measuring or an equipment failure, but everything checked out OK, and the reactions were repeated as we repeated the movement."

A mirror neuron is a brain cell which is active both when an animal performs an action and when the animal observes the same action performed by another animal. The neuron "mirrors" the behavior of another animal, as though the observer were himself performing the action. These neurons have been observed in primates, in some birds, and, yes, in humans, and scientists consider them to be one of the most important findings of neuroscience[32].

Have you ever watched a TV show where a character does

something incredibly embarrassing (like in pretty much every episode of *Curb Your Enthusiasm*) and felt yourself cringe in embarrassment on their behalf? Why do you do that? You have not done anything embarrassing and yet you feel as if you have. Mirror neurons may explain why you do that and why humans more generally share the feelings of those around them. They may be the biological basis for empathy and emotional contagion and why your happiness is deeply connected to everyone around you.

Social isolation/rejection causes pain

In one fascinating study, researchers put participants in an MRI scanner and made them play a simple game called Cyberball where players tossed a virtual ball between them. You can't throw real balls in an MRI scanner because you have to remain completely still during the scan.

Sometimes the other players would keep tossing the virtual ball between themselves, and keep a particular participant out of the game, causing the participant to feel socially rejected. The brain scans revealed that this made the participant's brain react the same way it would to physical pain[33]:

> *Being excluded from the game was associated with increased activation in the dACC and the AI, the very same areas involved in physical pain. Similar results have since been shown in other studies conducted in different labs.*

This again underscores that humans are intensely social and that one of the most important factors for happiness is good social relationships with other people[34].

Healthy brains know right from wrong

Scientists have even found that our brains seem wired to do the right thing[35]:

> *Studies indicate a "neuromoral" network for responding to moral dilemmas centered in the ventromedial prefrontal cortex and its connections, particularly on the right. The neurobiological evidence*

indicates the existence of automatic "prosocial" mechanisms for identification with others that are part of the moral brain. Patients with disorders involving this moral network have attenuated emotional reactions to the possibility of harming others and may perform sociopathic acts.

Being treated unfairly or seeing others suffer injustice causes negative emotions in most people, the notable exception being sociopaths and psychopaths who have no empathy and experience little or no negative emotions at the suffering of others. And crucially, this may be due to damage to their brains. I can't help but wonder how many of those cold, calculating, uncaring, "shareholder value first" leaders can act the way they do because of a brain malfunction.

One slightly scary research finding shows how much we value justice and possibly even revenge. A participant in an MRI scanner was playing a game in which they saw their opponent cheat them and get away with it. Later they saw the cheater receive an electric shock and this caused activation in the pleasure center of the brain of the test subject[36]. Apparently seeing cheaters get punished makes us feel good.

Positive surprises make us happy

According to research, we become happier when good things happen to us (shocking, I know!), but the effect is even bigger when good things happen to us unexpectedly:

Emory University and Baylor College of Medicine researchers used MRI brain scans to measure changes in human brain activity in response to a sequence of pleasurable stimuli.

They used a computer-controlled device to squirt fruit juice or water into the mouths of 25 research participants. The patterns of the squirting were either predictable or unpredictable.

The researchers found that the MRI scans showed a brain area called the nucleus accumbens to be much more active when the subjects received unpredictable patterns of juice and water.

The nucleus accumbens is an area of the brain highly involved in pleasure-seeking behavior and is typically active when we get a reward or expect something good to happen to us. So when something nice happens that you expect, it's good, but when nice things happens unexpectedly it's even better.

This chapter in tweets

- For the first time in human history, we have hard data on what makes us happy. Leaders need to know this research and apply it.
- Research clearly shows that there are ways to increase your own and other's happiness—both here and now and long-term.
- The best definition of happiness: The experience of positive well-being, combined with a sense that life is good, meaningful, and worthwhile.
- Emotions matter a lot—even at work. Frequent positive emotions make you smarter, healthier, and more successful.
- Study: happy people do better in three life domains—work, relationships, and health.
- Many people think that satisfaction and happiness are the same thing. This is a mistake.
- Emotions are contagious. Happy people lift the mood of everyone around them, and unhappy people bring everyone else down.
- Negativity bias affects everything. Our minds focus more on anything that's bad than on the good.
- Practice gratitude. If you're never grateful for what you have, it doesn't matter how much you have; it will never make you happy.
- Happiness is intensely social. Social isolation lights up the brain the same way physical pain does.
- We are born altruistic and empathetic. We get more happiness from pleasing others than from pleasing

ourselves. Workplaces should reflect this.

- Healthy brains know right from wrong. Disrespectful, egotistical jerk bosses may act the way they do because of a brain malfunction.
- The brain likes surprises. "Something nice happens that you expect" is good. "Something nice happens unexpectedly" is even better.

What is happy leadership

> *What drives me is to do right by other people and to serve them with excellence.*
>
> *If you're trying to help somebody else out, if you're trying to improve their lives, you work as hard as you can to accomplish that, driven by an inner need to help people—leadership basically consists of that.*
>
> *–Herb Kelleher*[37]

Let's use all the things we've looked at in the previous two chapters to define happy leadership more formally:

> *Happy leadership is simply leadership which has a net-positive effect and increases happiness in the world.*

The four main groups we should focus on are:

- The leader him- or herself
- Employees
- Customers
- The community/world

Leadership must be focused on happiness in two ways:

1. The goals the leader works towards should serve to increase the amount of happiness in the world
2. The leader should work towards those goals in a way that

promotes happiness in itself

Addressing only one of the two aspects is not enough. A leader who works for a good cause, but leads in a way that makes everyone around her miserable is not a good leader. Imagine the leader of a charity working to increase access to clean drinking water in rural Africa, who rules her team with an iron fist, abusing employees, vendors, and partners alike. No matter how noble the cause is, this is not happy leadership.

Conversely, imagine a CEO of a factory who genuinely loves his employees and treats them exceptionally well, but whose factory pollutes the environment in order to cut costs, harming the health of humans and animals in the area. Clearly this is wrong too.

Leaders by definition have a large influence on others and therefore a large responsibility to ensure that their leadership affects others positively. Fundamentally, leaders *must care* about the effect their leadership has on others. If a leader doesn't care how their leadership affects others, there is something very wrong with that person. Indeed, causing harm to others and not caring is one of the hallmarks of a sociopath.

It's not realistic to expect *every* goal a leader has or *every* action they take to improve happiness, but the end result of their leadership should be a net-positive in the world. Simply put, the world is in some big or small way a better, happier place, because of their leadership.

Traditional leadership	**Happy leadership**
Leadership is about living up to virtues like decisiveness, charisma, ambition, competitiveness, or similar.	Good leadership is defined by the effect it has on all who are affected by it. Good leadership has positive effects; bad leadership has negative effects.
Good leadership is about *me as a leader* achieving	Good leadership is about me and everyone affected

my goals and ambitions and goals. I can safely ignore how my leadership affects others.	by my leadership.
Good leadership is about maximizing business results. If I exploit employees, customers or the environment to achieve results, that's acceptable—maybe even admirable.	Good leadership aims to minimize suffering and maximize happiness for as many as possible.
Emotions have no role in the workplace—leave them at home.	Positive emotions have a huge effect on our wellbeing, health, and performance and are an integral part of work life.
It doesn't matter what makes people happy—leadership is about results.	Know the science, figure out what makes people happy or unhappy and lead accordingly. It's the right thing to do and leads to better results.

Imagine the pride and passion you as a leader can feel, knowing that your leadership is making people's lives better. Imagine a world where most business leaders think this way and actively practice their leadership in service not just of this month's sales targets, but in service of a better world. The potential is mind-boggling.

This is not only a wonderful ideal with huge potential for creating a better world; but this is also what leadership *should* be. If you cannot figure out how to lead in a way that is a net-positive in the world, then you should not be a leader. If a company can't figure out a way to operate that, on the whole, makes the world a better place, then that company should not be in business.

Ben Zander directly measures his success as a conductor by

the positive effect he has on those around him:

> *Doing well in the stock market, or satisfying the shareholders is a natural byproduct of an effective business. And what makes an effective business is the same thing that makes an effective orchestra: People who want to be there, who give everything they have, who are having a wonderful time doing it, whose eyes are shining, who are giving out energy to people around them.*
>
> *My definition of success is how many shining eyes do I have around me?*

How many shining eyes do you have around you?

What happy leadership is not

The challenge of using the word "happiness" in conjunction with anything work-related is that it gives some people the wrong idea. "So we're just going to have fun at work and never get any work done?" is a classic objection. Another is "But what if I have to give someone negative feedback? Won't that make them unhappy?"

So, let's also define what leading with happiness *isn't.*

It's not perfect eternal happiness

Maybe one of the biggest misunderstandings of happiness is that we should aim to be constantly happy. That is an impossible goal.

What we're aiming for is as much long-term happiness as possible for as many as possible—it's not about making sure that every single person is happy every single moment. This means that sometimes you do things that make people unhappy now but will increase happiness over time.

Addressing interpersonal conflict is a great example. If two of your employees have a long-standing conflict, you must address it. Calling them in for a meeting to resolve the conflict is unlikely to be fun for anyone, but the emotional cost of not addressing a conflict gets a lot higher down the road. Studies in conflict resolution find that the longer a conflict is allowed to go on, the harder it becomes to resolve.

Happy leadership is not about pleasing everyone all the time. Sometimes we do unpleasant things now, either because they must be done or because not doing them will cause even more unhappiness later. Fortunately, we're all used to these kinds of trade-offs and perform them all the time. I doubt that brushing your teeth or cleaning your home makes you happy, but you do it anyway because you know that losing all your teeth or living in a messy home will make you unhappy.

Also, people are different and, crucially, they are happy to different degrees and in quite different ways. Peter might be at his desk, quietly doing his job with a neutral expression on his face—but feeling pretty content nonetheless. Meanwhile, Susan is doing her job with high energy, a huge infectious smile on her face, and constantly interacting with the people around her—and clearly feeling happy too. Both of these are perfectly fine.

As we saw on page 19, everyone has a happiness set-point, and the goal of happy leadership is not to push everyone to be at an emotional 9 or 10 at all times. If a person's set-point is 5 or 6, that's going to be nearly impossible anyway. Rather the goal is to maximize happiness over time for as many people as possible and let each person live up to their happiness potential.

It's not about a comfortable or easy work life

When I met Garry Ridge, the CEO of the WD-40 Company, I, of course, wanted to learn more about this highly successful business, but I had one additional goal, which was to tell him the following joke:

> *Did you know that all problems in life can be solved with either WD-40 or duct tape?*
>
> *If something moves and it's not supposed to, use duct tape.*
>
> *If it doesn't move and it's supposed to, use WD-40.*

Sadly, he'd heard it before.

WD-40 Company has a strong culture, and while people are definitely happy at work there, this is not because work is easy, predictable, or comfortable. Quite the contrary, every single person there is expected to constantly do a great job, take responsibility for their own work life, and always challenge themselves to improve. This is codified in the WD-40 Maniac Pledge, which every new employee must take:

> *I am responsible for taking action, asking questions, getting answers, and making decisions.*
>
> *I won't wait for someone to tell me. If I need to know, I'm responsible for asking.*
>
> *I have no right to be offended that I didn't "get this sooner."*
>
> *If I'm doing something others should know about, I'm responsible for telling them.*

They recognize that being happy at work does not come when work is easy or simple, but when you are challenged and growing. The American psychologist Theodore Isaac Rubin put it like this:

> *Happiness does not come from doing easy work. It comes from the afterglow of satisfaction after the achievement of a difficult task that demands your best.*

It's not positive thinking

If you're wondering how *not* to create a happy workplace, here's an example:

> One German IT company came up with the perfect solution to combat whining in the workplace—it's made cheerfulness a contractual obligation. What's more, the CEO declared that those who weren't happy enough in the morning should stay home until they cheer up.

Some people take happiness to mean that you should *always* be happy. This is the idea of *Positive Thinking*—a poorly defined concept, which at its most extreme says that in every situation you can choose your own mood and your own reactions. No matter what happens to you, you can always choose a positive attitude[I].

"Fake it till you make it," they say, claiming that faking happiness actually makes you happier. Basically, if you don't feel happy every moment of your life, it's just your own damn fault for not trying hard enough.

Now, this idea is not completely unfounded. In many situations, you can actually change your mood and outlook through conscious effort. Let's say you're stuck in traffic on your way to work. In a situation like that, you can probably change your mindset and switch from being annoyed about the delay to a more positive interpretation of the situation. "Great, I have more time to listen to this interesting podcast," or something like that. Nothing wrong with that.

But the most fanatic proponents of positive thinking go much further. They claim that you can always change your thinking and that external circumstances don't matter at all. No matter what situation you're in, they say, you can simply choose to be happy.

Tell that to someone who's seriously ill, someone who's just been fired or someone who's suffering from severe depression. Actually, you should never tell them that, because telling someone in a rough life situation that they should think more positively is incredibly condescending and a terrible way to trivialize their pain. You could say I positively hate positive thinking.

Happy leadership is definitely not about forcing yourself or others to be happy because studies show that that actually backfires. German researchers set up an experiment to test what happens when we force people to fake being happy at work[38]:

> The team set up a fake railway customer complaints call center and asked 80 university students to take part in

I A quick note: One thing that bugs me is when people confuse positive thinking with positive psychology, which I wrote about back on page 18. They're not the same thing—the only thing they have in common is the word "positive".

> experiments while acting as staff. Half of the group were told that they could verbally defend themselves against rude customers, but the other half had to remain friendly and polite at all times.
>
> The volunteers' heart rates were measured, and preliminary results showed that the group that was allowed to verbally defend themselves had only a slightly increased heart rate. But the heart rates of the group who stayed polite shot up and continued to beat at a noticeably greater rate long after they had ended their telephone calls.
>
> Professor Zapf said, "Based on previous stress research, we know an increased heart rate can lead to cardiovascular problems and is a clear indicator of a higher psychological workload. It's about time we did away with the concept that the customer is always right and showed more respect for those in customer service jobs."
>
> "We call this kind of faked emotion 'emotional dissonance.' We found that the amount of time actually spent with customers was irrelevant when measuring stress compared to the amount of time workers had to demonstrate emotional dissonance."

So faking happiness actually makes us *less happy and more stressed.*

It's also worth reminding yourself that negative emotions are a natural part of work, as this story from an IT systems project manager demonstrates:

> I had a big client in France who couldn't make up their mind. In every single meeting, the customer changed the specs for the IT system that we were developing for them. First, they want this, then they want that. First, they want it this way, then that way. I try to explain that this is not a good way to work, but it still goes on. Meanwhile, I'm quietly going crazy.
>
> Finally, I lose my temper in a meeting. They introduce change number 283 (by my loose count), once again going back on what they've told me previously, and I snap. I actually pound the table with my fist, slam my project folder shut and say through clenched teeth "No. This can't go on. This system will never get off the ground if you keep changing your mind at every meeting. We need to make

decisions and stick to them".

In this situation, I felt AND showed anger—a negative emotion. I could've forced myself to be positive in that situation, but it would have been a betrayal of my work and myself, and it would have felt even worse. Not only was I authentic by being angry, that outburst finally got the client to respect me and established a much better working relationship going forward.

The thing to remember is that negative emotions are not called that because they're wrong, but simply because they're unpleasant. Sometimes a negative emotion is exactly the right emotion, and if you're always forcing yourself to be positive, you're being both less authentic and less effective. When your circumstances are bad, there is nothing wrong with being unhappy; it is only natural. It's an excellent motivator to do something about it.

Another reason why positive thinking is bad is that it can contribute to quelling dissent and ignoring problems in the workplace. Ever heard someone say "In this workplace, we don't have problems, only opportunities?" I hate that phrase with a vengeance, partly because it's wrong but mostly because it's so often used to stifle dissent and criticism. No workplace is perfect. No job is without problems. If we consistently marginalize and criticize people who are unhappy at work by telling them to be positive and never complain, we lose some very valuable voices of reason and realism in the workplace.

Finally, and most importantly, positive thinking just doesn't work. An excellent article from Harvard Business Review examined the science behind positive thinking and concluded that:

> *...across dozens of peer-reviewed studies examining the effects of positive visions of the future on people pursuing various kinds of wishes —from health-related, such as losing weight, quitting smoking, or recovering quickly from surgery, to the improvement of professional or academic performance (for example, mid-level managers wishing to reduce job-related stress, graduate students looking for a job, or*

school children seeking to get good grades) —we've consistently found that people who positively fantasize make either the same or less progress in achieving attainable wishes than those who don't.[39]

Happy leadership is not about faking happiness or demanding that everyone be happy at all times. It's about being emotionally authentic and recognizing that negative emotions are an integral and important part of work life.

This chapter in tweets

- Achieving business success is nothing noble or admirable in itself. What counts is doing it in a way that makes the world better.
- You lead with happiness when you: 1) Work for goals that make the world better. 2) Work towards those goals in a way that promotes happiness.
- Imagine the pride and passion happy leaders can feel, knowing that their leadership is making people's lives better.
- If you cannot figure out how to lead in a way that is a net-positive in the world, then you should not be a leader.
- One of the biggest misunderstandings of happiness is that we should aim to be constantly happy. That is an impossible goal.
- Talking about "happiness" at work gives some people the wrong idea, e.g., "So we're just going to have fun at work and never get any work?"
- Being happy at work does not come when work is easy or simple, but when we are challenged and growing.
- Happy leadership is not about forcing yourself or others to be happy—studies show that that actually backfires.
- Happiness can't be faked—it must be genuine.

Happy leaders start with themselves

> *I know I'm fortunate to live an extraordinary life, and that most people would assume my business success, and the wealth that comes with it, have brought me happiness. But they haven't; in fact, it's the reverse. I am successful, wealthy and connected because I am happy.*
>
> *–Richard Branson*

Now that we've looked at the science and philosophy of happiness and used that to define what happy leadership is and isn't, it's time to look at how it's done. Specifically, the next few chapters will show how happy leaders create more happiness for four main constituencies: For themselves, for their employees, for the customers, and for the world.

If you want to make others happier, you have to start with yourself. As Charlie Kim, the CEO of Next Jump, told me: "You can't give to others, what you don't have yourself."

Imagine a leader who genuinely loves her job. She is engaged in the work itself and enjoys doing it. She likes her people, knows them well and sees and appreciates their qualities. She has a clear sense that her work is meaningful and makes a positive difference in the world. She is not perfectly happy every second of every day (no one is), but she comes to work most days with passion, enthusiasm, and a smile on her face. Most days, she leaves the workplace fulfilled and energized after another great workday. While she loves her job, she doesn't work herself to death, making sure that there's always time for her family, friends, and hobbies.

This is what being a leader should be like, and it's not only good for the leader herself, it has a direct influence on employee happiness and business results. Research shows that happy leaders:

- Make better decisions.
- Prioritize scarce resources better.
- Manage their time better.
- Have more empathy for others.
- Are more optimistic.
- Make their employees happier.
- Achieve more business success.

That last point is crucial. Many people think that happiness comes from being successful. Their belief is that "I will work really hard," they say. "That will make me successful in my leadership career and success will make me happy." While there is some truth to that, research shows that the link is much stronger in the other direction: People who are happy on average achieve more career success and higher lifetime incomes. So, leaders don't have to choose between success and happiness. It's about realizing that the two go hand in hand.

The aim of this chapter is not to tell you how to be happy. Everyone is different and what works for other people might not work for you at all. The aim is merely to show you, that you should value your own happiness and then to give you some inspiration for things that might work.

Get happy at work yourself

A 2005 study of health care workers by researchers from the University of Minnesota found that[40]:

> *Managers who were enthusiastic positively affected their employees' emotions.*

Employees of unhappy managers experienced less happiness, enthusiasm and optimism, and experienced a slight increase in irritation, anger, and anxiety.

A manager's leadership behaviors affect employees' emotions throughout the workday, even when the employees are not interacting with the managers.

If you, as a leader, are currently not happy at work, that is where you must start. As long as you are unhappy at work, you are likely to bring everyone else down through emotional contagion (see page 26). Even if you can hypothetically avoid spreading your misery to others (which is hard enough in itself), a situation where you spread happiness around you while remaining unhappy yourself, is just not sustainable.

Furthermore, not only will your unhappiness at work infect those around you in the workplace, it can have terrible negative effects on your private life. Studies show that people who are unhappy at work are:

- Less happy in life[41].
- More likely to gain weight[42].
- Less happy in their marriage/relationship[43].
- More prone to stress and depression[44].
- More at risk for heart disease[45] and strokes[46].
- More at risk for some forms of cancer[47].

Simply put, being unhappy at work can ruin your private life and your health, and it can ultimately kill you. So if you are not happy at work, there are two choices open to you; Do something to become happier in your current position or find a different job, where you can be happy. The only option not open to you is to do nothing. The second of these choices is the tough one, primarily because there are strong social biases against quitting. But if you've honestly tried to make yourself happy in your current job and it just does not seem to work, then it may be time to move on[II].

II We run a website called www.InternationalQuitYourCrappyJobDay.com that may help.

If you're happy and you know it...

Research clearly shows that leaders are generally happier than their employees. In 2014, the Pew Research Center found that in the US, 69% of bosses were "very satisfied" with their jobs but only 48% of workers said the same thing. When the survey looked at home life, the difference was still there, but noticeably smaller: 83% of bosses describe themselves as "very satisfied" with their family situation compared to 74% of workers[48].

Why would leaders be happier? They work longer hours on average, have more responsibility, and are more socially isolated than employees. Shouldn't that make them more stressed and less happy? Or is it just that managers make more money and that makes them happier?

A European study based on data from 2006/7 showed some of the answers. It first agreed that there is a "substantial satisfaction gap between those holding managerial positions and workers." It then concludes that the difference is largely due to the fact that leaders have more autonomy, more influence over the firm's decisions, and more opportunities to learn[49]. Once you control for these factors, the satisfaction gap between managers and workers almost disappears.

So, leaders enjoy more freedom and control and that on average makes them happier than their employees. However, many leaders are afraid to show that they're happy. They feel that leaders shouldn't be happy; they should be *serious, competent,* and *professional.*

So, if you, as a leader, are already happy, why not make an effort to show it? You can do things like:

- Smile and be positive
- See and appreciate the good things in the workplace
- See and appreciate the good qualities in your people
- Express optimism

You should *not* fake being happy if you aren't. As we saw on page 43, that actually backfires. Find your own genuine and authentic way to be happy and to express it.

Move

Most of us spend most of the workday sitting down. We sit at our desks, we sit in meetings, we sit down at lunch, we sit down for seminars, phone calls, orientations, and just about anything else that goes on during a typical work week. A New York Times article reported that this gives us:

> *...an increased risk of obesity, diabetes, heart disease, a variety of cancers and an early death. In other words, irrespective of whether you exercise vigorously, sitting for long periods is bad for you.*

We all knew that sitting down all day is bad for you, but I at least thought that you could offset this with exercise outside of work. I was wrong.

The article goes on to list two reasons why physical inactivity is so bad for your health. First, it's passive which means your body burns very few calories while you sit. Just standing up activates your system to a much larger degree and burns more energy. But it doesn't stop there:

> *When you spend long periods sitting, your body actually does things that are bad for you. Actively contracting muscles produce a whole suite of substances that have a beneficial effect on how the body uses and stores sugars and fats.*
>
> *A study of people who sit for many hours found that those who took frequent small breaks —standing up to stretch or walk down the corridor—had smaller waists and better profiles for sugar and fat metabolism than those who did their sitting in long, uninterrupted chunks*[50].

Moving is also great for your mind[51], giving you overall improved cognitive performance, including:

- Improved concentration
- Sharper memory
- Faster learning
- Prolonged mental stamina

- Enhanced creativity
- Lower stress
- Improved mood

Leaders who are physically active and healthy are more likely to be happy, but it's important to get this straight: The science does not show that you must run a half-marathon every day. The main health benefits actually come from moving often throughout the day.

While actual exercise is definitely also good for you, don't just do it because you have to. Find a form of exercise that you truly enjoy that you can do together with others. One researcher gave this recommendation[52]:

> *We need to have people do things that they absolutely love, that bring them great joy and pride and build their self-confidence, and things that make them feel less alone and more a part of a larger community working on something that all participants value.*

Sleep

> *"I'm a huge advocate for sleep, and I prioritize it the same way I would prioritize going to the gym and seeing my friends. I aim for eight hours a night but probably get closer to seven. It's so hard because it's the thing that seems the easiest to sacrifice."*
>
> *-Mana Ionescu, president of Lightspan Digital, a Chicago-based digital marketing agency[53].*

Some leaders subscribe to a macho ideal that sleep is for wimps. They may brag about how little sleep they're getting as if it's something to be proud of when in reality sleep deprivation has tremendous costs[54]:

> *Sleep deprivation is associated with considerable social, financial, and health-related costs. Cognitive functions particularly affected by sleep loss include psychomotor and cognitive speed, vigilant and*

executive attention, working memory, and higher cognitive abilities.

Chronic sleep-restriction experiments—which model the kind of sleep loss experienced by many individuals with sleep fragmentation and premature sleep curtailment due to disorders and lifestyle—demonstrate that cognitive deficits accumulate to severe levels over time without full awareness by the affected individual.

About 1% of the population is genetically predisposed to need very little sleep, but you are probably not one of them. In fact, as the quote above shows, sleep deprivation may be hurting you, without you even being aware of it. This has direct implications for leaders.

Leaders who sleep well, lead well. This is the direct finding from a small but fascinating study on sleep quality in leaders[55]. Each morning for two weeks, 88 leaders filled out a survey on how long and how well they'd slept the previous night. Their employees filled out a different survey at the end of the workday about any abusive behavior from their boss and their work engagement that day. One of the researchers behind the study, Cristopher M. Barnes, sums it up like this:

Although most of us have some appreciation that our own sleep influences our own behaviors and outcomes, not many people would expect someone else's sleep to influence one's own behavior. But this is precisely what we found; leader sleep quality influenced subordinate work engagement. Thus, if leaders want their subordinates to be truly engaged, they should start by looking at their own sleep.

Charlie Kim, the CEO of IT company Next Jump, takes this so seriously that he's introduced sleep to the office[56]:

Most company executives would say that they are not responsible for helping how much sleep an employee gets —that's a personal issue. We at Next Jump feel the opposite.

We saw that as our leadership development programs grew (and people gained more responsibility), people couldn't sleep—they simply couldn't shut their minds off. The dynamic was clear—more senior, more responsibility... less sleep.

We tried nap rooms but found they didn't work. The availability of a welcoming bed didn't address the main problem of why staff members weren't able to sleep. They couldn't shut their minds off.

In the last six months, we experimented to find a different solution, and we have now rolled out a daily 30-minute sleep class from 2:30 to 3:00 pm in all our offices.

The message for leaders is clear:

1. Make sure you get enough sleep—most people need 7–8 hours. Go to bed earlier, get up later or find time to sleep during the day, whatever works for you.
2. Sleep better. I won't try to tell you how—it's different for everyone. Experiment with ways to improve your sleep quality.

Practice gratitude

Don't ruin the things you have by wanting what you don't have, but realize that they too were things you once wished for.

–Epicurus

As we saw on page 29, one of the keys to happiness is to appreciate the good things we already have. This makes perfect sense; if a person never appreciates the good things they have, it doesn't matter how many good things they have because they're always focused on getting more, rather than on feeling grateful for what they have.

While I haven't seen any research to support this, it does seem to me that many leaders fall into that particular trap. They see themselves as *ambitious*, *driven*, and *competitive*, so while they may work hard to achieve certain goals and results, they never seem to enjoy them once they have them. Instead, their focus is constantly on the next goal, i.e., on what they *don't have*.

For some, it's even a point of pride. Old-style leaders proudly say things like "I am never satisfied. I always want more, and that ambition is the key to my success." This is clearly misguided for two reasons. First of all, what's the point of achieving success, if one never enjoys it but is always just driven to want *more*? Secondly, these leaders fall into the "suffering leads to success" trap (which we will cover on page 160), when we know that happy people, in fact, are more successful on average.

So, practice becoming aware of and feeling grateful for the good things in your work life. Here are some ways to do it:

- Every Friday afternoon, make a list of 3–5 good things that happened at work.
- Think of someone who has helped you grow personally or professionally at work and call or write to thank that person.
- Think of someone you really enjoy working with and thank that person.
- Make a list of five things you like about your job.
- Think of the best leader you've ever worked for. Thank that person.

Maintain your relationships

As we've seen again and again (going all the way back to Epicurus), humans are social beings. No one is happy in isolation—even introverts are generally happier when they're around other people[57]. Many people think that being a leader automatically means cutting yourself off from others. "It's cold at the top," is a classic bone-headed maxim and "You can't make friends at work," is another. A Norwegian study of 3,000 managers exposed how wrong that is, concluding[58]:

> *Managers experience significantly less stress when they feel they have a good relationship with their*

employees, and the employees show a positive conduct and confidence in their managers.

The best thing a manager can do to prevent work stress is to develop good relationships with the employees at work.

One of the most important things you can do as a leader is to have great relationships with your employees. This does not mean being best friends with every single employee, but it does mean having a respectful and trusting mutual relationship. We will look more at how to do that in the next chapter. And of course, relationships are hugely important in private life too. As we saw on page 30, happiness is intensely social. Having deep, loving, long-lasting relationships outside of work with your spouse/partner, friends, children, parents, and wider family is crucial to your own happiness. Too many leaders sacrifice love on the altar of business success.

Get advice

When I met Jiři Halousek, the CEO and founder of the IT company Iresoft in the Czech Republic, he had a startling admission: "Three years ago, I was an asshole." He explained that he used to be a hard-nosed, demanding leader who made his employees and himself miserable—but never realized it. Finally one of his friends suggested that he get a business coach to help him change his behavior and, reluctantly, he did. The first few sessions were tough because he essentially didn't want to do it, but gradually Jiři came to see the value of the process and found ways to change his behavior for the better. He explained the results like this:

One of the most crucial things I have changed is to trust people. Earlier, I did not trust people, and they behaved accordingly. I realized that most people are good and can be trusted and when my colleagues saw this, they did not want to disappoint me. I, as the leader, had to be the first one to offer trust between us. The other way round does not work.

I am now much happier and relaxed at work, my employees are happier and more productive, and I don't feel completely isolated in the company like all the responsibility is on my shoulders alone. Oh, and the company is doing better and growing faster.

Changing behaviors is much easier if you get some help from a good coach, mentor, friend, or someone similar who can help you define your goals and make sure you act constructively to achieve them.

Stop and think

Teresa Amabile, a professor at Harvard Business School, and Steven Kramer, a psychologist and researcher, conducted a big research project on how happiness at work affects productivity by making subjects keep a journal of their work life. Every day, the subjects would get an email with some questions about their day. One question asked people to briefly report one event that stood out in their minds from the workday. Here's what they found[59]:

Although this question simply asked for an event—a concrete description of something specific that happened and who was involved—we found that, very often, people didn't stop there. They told us, sometimes in great detail, about their perceptions of the event and the thoughts that it engendered. They told us about how the event made them feel. And sometimes they told us how it affected their motivation and performance that day.

Analyzing the data they gathered clearly showed Amabile and Kramer how our emotions affect our productivity, creativity, and resilience, but there was an additional accidental finding: *Journaling itself has some very positive effects*[60].

Sarah Kaus, the founder of a company called S'Well that makes insulated drinking bottles, explains what she gets out of keeping a journal:

Journaling about work has given me the focus to identify my strengths and the activities that bring me the greatest joy. I have gleaned many lessons about where I can be most engaged and therefore most successful in the workplace. Journaling has also given me patience and sharpened my ability to plan.

I am always encouraged to look back and know how far I have come in a year's time, and how major obstacles seem to become minor speed bumps in hindsight. This record gives me great patience and perspective when new challenges come my way. Even now as a very busy entrepreneur, I can't imagine not taking a few moments at the end of each day to record in my journal the progress made and my hopes and plans for the next phases of success.

Leaders are busy almost by definition. I've met bosses whose every moment for the next three weeks has already been booked for meetings, leaving no free time for reflection and thought. I always tell them: "Remember you're a leader—not a meeter."

The fascinating book "Scarcity: Why Having Too Little Means So Much" by professor of economics Sendhil Mullainathan and professor of psychology Eldar Shafir, clearly shows the negative cognitive effects of time scarcity. Simply put, not having enough time makes you less intelligent, more vulnerable to temptation, and worse at effectively managing what little time you do have[61]. How do you avoid it? By actively planning some free time during your day, says Shafir:

When you're dealing with a scarcity of time, plan a few moments of slack throughout the day — a half-hour here or there intentionally left open so that if anything comes up you can avail yourself of that unaccounted-for time and take care of the thing you hadn't anticipated. I call it having a meeting with yourself.

In his article "In Praise of Slack: Time Is of the Essence" from The Academy of Management Executives, M. B. Lawson also underscores the importance of having free time during your workday that is not already taken up with tasks because you need time to deal with new complex issues[62]:

> *Increasingly complex systems and technologies require more, not less, time for monitoring and processing information. Future demands for strategic flexibility and for integrating learning and knowledge throughout organizations highlight the need to reexamine the importance of time in organizational work—and to recognize that all organizational resources cannot be committed to immediate output efforts if we are to have time to pay attention, think and benefit from the knowledge gained.*

Do you ever stop and think or are you always busy meeting and working? Here are some ways to do it:

- Keep a daily or weekly work journal. Just before you go home from work, write down one paragraph of observations about your day/week.
- Take five minutes of Me-Time daily. Go somewhere you won't be disturbed and take a few moments to reflect on what's happening and how you feel today.
- Meet regularly with one or more peers for common reflection time.

SEB Pension in Copenhagen picked the last one. All leaders are required to have a buddy and meet with them every other week. Every person picks one theme they'd like to improve on and then use the biweekly meetings to evaluate and support each others' progress. Their Head of Legal, Helene Neergaard, told me that she is currently focused on the theme of *giving feedback* and how this regular reflection time has helped her directly by:

- Getting tips and ideas from her peers.
- Getting clarity on her goals and her progress towards achieving them.
- Forming deeper workplace relationships through sharing their challenges and success.

Don't overwork

CNN asked 12 well-known leaders including Carlos Ghosn of Nissan, Marissa Mayer of (then) Google, and famous jazz musician Wynton Marsalis how they manage their time and stay efficient[63]. My favorite answer is this one:

> *I know that it's normal for executives to start the day extremely early, but frankly, I feel I make better decisions and relate better to people when I'm well rested. So, I usually get up around 7.30 after a good night's sleep.*
>
> *I also make sure to work a standard 40-hour week and rarely work on weekends. This is important to me for two reasons. First of all, I have a life outside of work. I have a family who likes to have me around and friends and hobbies that I also want to have time for. I find that the time I spend outside of work recharges my batteries, expands my horizons and actually makes me more efficient at work.*
>
> *Secondly, if I'm always seen arriving at the office at 6 in the morning and leaving at 9 in the evening, not to mention taking calls and writing emails late at night and all weekend, it's sure to send a signal to my employees that this is what the company expects, that this is "the right way". But it isn't.*
>
> *It's a simple fact that for most leaders and employees, the first 40 hours they work each week are worth much more to the company than the next 20, 30 or, 40 hours. But those extra hours spent at work can harm your private life, your family, and your health. Which in turn becomes damaging to the company.*
>
> *Frankly, if you can't structure your time so your work fits inside a 40-hour week, you need to get better at prioritizing and delegating.*

Refreshing words. Guess which of the executives said that?

Come on, take a guess!

NONE OF THEM! Not one.

Instead, there's a lot of "I get up at 5 and arrive at the office at 6", "I work 16 hours a day", "I take a lot of calls on the drive in to the office", and "I usually leave the office at 7 and then work a few more hours in the evening at home."

I fully expected one of them to say "I get up at 4 in the morning, half an hour before I go to bed, and work a 27-hour day, only stopping for a 3-minute lunch break in which two assistants stuff food down my throat like a foie-gras goose."

Leaders work a lot. One study of 483 executives, managers, and professionals found that[64]:

> *60% of those who carry smartphones for work are connected to their jobs 13.5 or more hours a day on weekdays and about five hours on weekends, for a total of about 72 hours [a week].*

I know it's normal to view people working this hard as heroes of the organization, but research shows they would be more efficient *and* enjoy life more if they cut down their time at work. They would be more open, less stressed, have more fun, and be better role models for their employees. You could even argue the opposite: Leaders who can't do their jobs in a regular 40-hour work week must be either incredibly unproductive, bad at managing their time, or terrible at delegating.

Cutting down working hours can even lead to *better* results, as this story from Arlie Hochschild's excellent book "The Time Bind" demonstrates:

> One executive, Doug Strain, the vice chairman of ESI, a computer company in Portland, Oregon, saw the link between reduced hours for some and more jobs for others. At a 1990 focus group for CEOs and managers, he volunteered the following story:
>
> When demand for a product is down, normally a company fires some people and makes the rest work twice as hard. So, we put it to a vote of everyone in the plant. We asked them what they wanted to do: layoffs for some workers or thirty-two-hour workweeks for everyone. They thought about it and decided they'd rather hold the team together. So, we

> went down to a thirty-two-hour-a-week schedule for everyone during a downtime. We took everybody's hours and salary down—executives too.
>
> But Strain discovered two surprises.
>
> First, productivity did not decline. I swear to God, we get as much out of them at thirty-two hours as we did at forty. So, it's not a bad business decision. But second, when economic conditions improved, we offered them one hundred percent time again. No one wanted to go back!
>
> Never in our wildest dreams would our managers have designed a four-day week. But it's endured at the insistence of our employees.

Temporary overwork is fine—it can even be fun to work hard and intensely for an important goal over a short period—but permanent overwork is bad for two reasons. First, it can kill you. One study found that "those working a 55-hour week face 33% increased risk of stroke than those working a 35- to 40-hour week."[65] Secondly, we *get no more work done*. An article in the Harvard Business Review titled "The Research Is Clear: Long Hours Backfire for People and for Companies" put it very clearly[66]:

> *Overwork doesn't seem to result in more output.*

If you think this doesn't apply to you, there's a simple reason. People who permanently overwork think they're getting a lot of work done and their self-reported productivity is through the roof. However, when their work output is measured objectively, it turns out they get less work done than peers who work regular hours. They also feel more stressed and make more mistakes in their work.

The school of "work your butt off, everything else comes second" is bad for business and bad for people. Permanent overwork kills people while not improving business results. Can we agree that it is dumb and leaders should stop doing it to themselves and their workers?

One leader who got this was the former US vice president, Joe Biden who sent this memo to his staff in 2014 telling them not to sacrifice their private lives for work:

"To my wonderful staff,

I would like to take a moment and make something clear to everyone. I do not expect, nor do I want any of you to miss or sacrifice important family obligations for work. Family obligations include, but are not limited to family birthdays, anniversaries, weddings, any religious ceremonies such as first communions and bar mitzvahs, graduations and times of need such as an illness or a loss in the family. This is very important to me. In fact, I will go so far as to say that if I find out you are working with me while missing important family responsibilities, it will disappoint me greatly. This has been an unwritten rule since my days in the Senate.

Thank you for all the hard work.

Sincerely,

Joe."

This chapter in tweets

- If you, as a leader, want to make others happier, you have to start with yourself. Unhappy leaders make everyone else miserable too.
- Research: happy leaders make better decisions, manage their time better, empathize more, and are more successful.
- People think success will make them happy. Studies show the opposite: Happy people work better and become more successful.
- Leaders who can't do their jobs without working 60 hours a week must be either unproductive, bad at managing time, or terrible at delegating.
- Study: managers' behaviors affect employees' emotions throughout the workday, even when the employees are not interacting with the managers.

- Leaders who have good relationships with their employees are happier and less stressed.
- Many leaders are happy but are afraid to show it thinking they should be serious, competent, and professional instead. You can be both!
- Don't sit down all day at work. Physical activity improves concentration, memory, creativity, energy, and health. Move!
- Some leaders think sleep is for wimps. But sleep deprivation makes you stressed, unhappy, dumber, and unhealthy.
- Practice gratitude for the good in your work life. Make a weekly list of 3–5 things that made you happy at work that week.
- Having deep, long-lasting relationships outside of work is crucial to happiness. Too many leaders sacrifice love on the altar of success.
- Changing behaviors is easier with help from a coach or mentor to define your goals and act on them.
- Some bosses' calendars are booked solid with meetings for weeks. Reminder: You're a leader—not a meeter.
- Studies: permanent overwork kills people and results in no increased output. Stop the cult of overwork.

Happiness for employees

It has to be job one. It can't slip to being job two, three, four or five. Because then you've lost it.

No matter how busy you get, taking care of your employees, being interested in your employees, communicating with your employees, honoring your employees is still job one.

–Herb Kelleher[67]

Herb Kelleher, the founder of Southwest Airlines and the company's CEO for 30 years, was very clear on his strategic priorities:

1. **Employees** come first, because when they are happy they do better work.
2. That makes the **customers** happy because they get great service at great prices.
3. That makes the **stockholders** happy because the customers keep coming back and the company makes more money.

Remarkably, this philosophy has led to an unbroken streak of profitability. Southwest is the only major airline in the world to have turned a profit every year since the 1970s.

Your employees are the people most directly affected by your leadership. As a leader, you have a huge opportunity to make your employees' lives richer, more meaningful, and more fun.

It's not that you *first* make yourself happy at work and *then* move on to your employees. The two should go hand in hand. Focusing on your own happiness while ignoring that of your employees is likely to backfire because no good manager can be happy while their employees are miserable.

In this chapter, we're going to look at ways for leaders to make their employees happy at work. But first, here's a general introduction to the most important things any leader should know about happiness at work.

What you should know about happy employees

Happiness at work is good for people

How people feel at work has a huge effect on them, not just at work but also in private life. People who are happy at work:

- Are happier in life.
- Have better marriages/relationships.
- Are healthier physically and mentally.
- Experience less stress.
- Live longer.

This is hardly surprising, given that we spend so much of our lives at work. Time Studies show that people on average spend the most time on sleep over their entire lives and work comes second. This means that we spend more of our waking hours at work than we do on anything else. When you spend that much of your life on anything, it really should be something you enjoy. If not, you're wasting your life.

Anyone can be happy at work

> Some years ago, I met a young man who worked in the sewers of Copenhagen—and believe it or not, he loved his job. He was the first to admit that working in the sewers was dirty and smelly, but he was happy at work anyway for two reasons. First, he was proud of the work he did because he knew that a well-functioning sewer system is so important for a city. And secondly, he was part of a great work team who helped each other and had a lot of fun at work.

There is a persistent myth that happiness at work is only for some people. Some people think that only highly skilled professionals (doctors, lawyers, engineers, and the like) can love their jobs while people doing manual labor can't. I've heard people say that only office workers can like work and blue-collar factory workers are doomed to be unhappy. Others again think that happiness at work is only for bosses and not for employees or only for people with high salaries. This happens to be completely wrong, and it's important for leaders to realize that happiness at work is not just for some employees. Anyone can be happy at work.

Salaries, titles, and perks can't make employees happy

Here's a partial list of perks that I've seen companies offer their employees to keep them happy and engaged: Free fruit, Office gyms, Fancy office design, Office parties, Competitions, Teambuilding activities, Wellness programs, Massages, Laundry/dry cleaning service, Legal counseling, Health insurance, Free breakfasts, Swimming pools, Christmas presents, Stop smoking programs, Weight loss programs, Nap pods, and Free drinks/coffee. Am I missing any?

Companies spend huge amounts on perks like these, but they make employees no happier at work because they target satisfaction rather than happiness. On the one hand, this is frustrating. Things would be so much easier if employee happiness was just a matter of putting in a gym and offering massages. On the other hand, it's great news because if it were so, only very wealthy workplaces, which could afford all of these pricey perks, could ever be happy. Luckily, the things that really make us happy at work are available on any budget.

However, we can't ignore compensation, titles, and perks completely, because even though they can't make employees happy, they can make them unhappy when they're unfair. If you want to see how important fairness is, try this experiment: Get two Capuchin monkeys, and train them to do a task (to give you back a small, polished rock) in exchange for a slice of cucumber. These are smart monkeys—they quickly learn that when they hand back the rock, they get their treat.

Then try something new: Give one of them a better treat than the other. Capuchin monkeys like cucumber fine, but they like grapes even better because they're sweeter. If one capuchin sees you paying the other one in grapes, it will refuse to cooperate, and will no longer hand over the rock in exchange for cucumber. "Listen, buster," it seems to say, "you're paying that guy in grapes, and my work is at least as good. I want grapes too, or I'm going on strike." Some of the monkeys even throw the now unwanted cucumber piece right back in the researcher's face.

We saw on page 34 that unfairness lights up the human brain in the same way as physical pain. We hate it. We want to be treated fairly, and we want to see others around us treated fairly as well.

This means that salaries, bonuses, titles, and perks do matter for our happiness at work because they can make us unhappy if we perceive them to be unfair. However, the same factors cannot make us happy at work. Once they're fair, increasing them further does not make people any happier at work. Many companies don't know this and try to create a better workplace environment through things like free smoothies, office gyms, and bonus schemes, which is bound to fail. We need to ensure that these things are fair and equitable and then go on to focus on the things that actually do make people happy at work.

Results and relationships make us happy at work

There's been a huge amount of research done into what makes people happy at work and I believe the findings can best be condensed like this:

The two major factors that make us happy at work are *results* and *relationships.*

Let's take a closer look at these two. First, results. Some leaders hold the view that people are inherently lazy and will do nothing if the leader isn't there to constantly put pressure and motivate employees to work hard. This view is antiquated and wrong. When given half a chance, people work their hearts out to accomplish results. We all want to make a difference, create value, know that our work is important, feel needed, and do work that we can be proud of.

People love to do great work and to make a difference. Accomplishment feels great. And it's also in the company's best interest to make sure that every single employee and team is getting great results and living up to their potential. Companies typically give employees some of these things to help them do their work well:

- **Skills:** Training, competencies, job skills match,...
- **Resources:** Time, tools, IT-systems, budgets,...
- **Structure:** Organization, plans, goals, strategy, processes,...
- **Support:** Coworker and manager support, coaches, mentors,...

These are all important and enable employees to get results. If leaders don't give employees these things, then how on earth can they be expected to perform well?

If we want people to be happier at work, we can definitely help them get better results. We can give them better training, more resources, more support, and the like to help them perform better. However, many employees already get good results but *don't feel that way*. And if that's the case, they won't be very happy at work. Because happiness is emotional in nature, it is not the actual objectively measurable results an employee achieves that makes them happier but their *feeling of results*. If, for instance, an employee does good work but is never recognized for it or can't see why that work is meaningful, that employee may never have a feeling of results and accomplishment.

This is a crucial distinction leaders need to know—the distinction between *getting good results* and *feeling good about those results*. If we want employees to be happy at work, they also need the latter. If that is not the case, employees may get great results right now, but it won't be sustainable. When people are not happy at work, it hurts their motivation, productivity, and creativity. Stress and burnout tend to follow.

So, in addition to helping employees get great results, companies also need to make sure that people *feel great* about their results. There are three things leaders must give employees, that let them *feel* that they get great results at work:

- **Autonomy:** When people have control and freedom at work, they are happier and take more pride in the results they create because they did it *their way*.
- **Meaning and purpose:** This lets them see that their work matters and makes a positive difference. They know not just *what* they're doing but *why* they're doing it.
- **Feedback:** This makes them feel recognized and appreciated for their work and also shows how they can improve.

We're going to look at each of these later in this chapter.

Which brings us to relationships at work. As we saw on page 30, happiness is inherently social and highly dependent on the depth and quality of our relationships. Relationships at work matter so much because we spend a lot of time with the other people in our workplaces. When you think about it, you'll be spending more of your waking hours with them, than with your friends and family combined.

The single scariest study I have ever seen in this field showed just how crucial workplace relationships are: A study of 800 Israelis found that people with bad workplace relationships had a 240% increased risk of dying from heart disease over a 20-year period[68].

As we saw on page 56, leaders who have good relationships with their employees are happier and less stressed themselves, and there is equally clear evidence that employees who have a good relationship with their immediate manager are happier and more productive at work. Now, I'm not saying that you have to be best friends with all of your employees; what you should have is a good working relationship, where your people know that you have time for them, care about them, know them, and treat them with respect. We're going to look at some ways to do this later in the chapter. Good relations don't have to stop with co-workers and managers but can also apply to customers, suppliers, shareholders, and the surrounding community.

These two factors—results and relationships—are universal because they represent our two deepest psychological needs:

- Results: The need to contribute, make a difference and control our environment
- Relationships: The need to belong to a group and feel accepted and liked as a person

They are built into us so deeply, that they hold true across all cultures, across all types of employees, for men and women, and for young and old employees. This also means that if you, as a leader, want to be happy at work, you need them in your own work life. Can you honestly say that you have great results and relationships at work?

Where is your focus?

Between results and relationships, which do you focus on the most? Are you mostly focused on getting results or creating relationships at work? What about your workplace as a whole? Does it mostly emphasize and strive for results or relationships? Think about it for a second.

It's probably safe to say that the majority of business leaders focus most on results. This is hardly surprising—organizations exist for the results they create. They're all about the budgets, plans, projects, strategies, and missions, i.e., the results. So, it's perfectly understandable that leaders should focus so much on results. It's also a mistake.

What often happens is that many leaders focus so much on results that they forget about relationships at work. But good relationships don't come by themselves; it takes a concerted, daily effort to create them. When this is neglected, relationships at work go bad. Instead of teamwork and mutual appreciation, there is mistrust, internal conflict, bickering, and selfishness.

This of course makes people unhappy at work, and when people are unhappy at work, results suffer. Which of course makes the workplace focus *even more* on results. Ironically, focusing too much on results *harms results!*

And that is why leaders must focus equally on results and

relationships in everything they do. Here are some examples:

Activity	Results	Relationships
Meetings	Have a clear agenda, have only the right people there, and let everyone contribute.	Make the meeting fun, listen to everyone, let new people introduce themselves, and make time for small talk.
Hiring	Look for people with the right professional and personal skills to do the job well.	Look for people who will fit into the team and culture.
Projects	Have clear goals, plans, and deadlines.	Create a great project team, where people like each other and work well together.

In business, it is common to primarily acknowledge results-oriented managers, instead of those with strong social skills. Usually, the most professionally competent employees are promoted to managerial positions, even if they lack the social skills that make a good manager. If these new managers do not get the training/further education they need, it has a direct negative impact on happiness at work and consequently on productivity.

We need to challenge that thinking because leaders are far more successful if they have excellent relationship skills. Of course, leaders need to have a focus on results too, but it is probably much easier for a person with good social skills to learn to focus on results than it is for a hard-core results-driven person to develop social skills and empathy.

Southwest Airlines have long done this. The excellent book "The Southwest Airlines Way" by Jody Hoffer-Gittell reveals one of the secrets to Southwest's remarkable success: they have great relationships that create an enormous competitive advantage in motivation, teamwork, and coordination among Southwest employees. For instance, when Southwest looks for new managers, the most important skill is the ability to connect with others and create good relationships[69].

On the most basic level, happy leaders care about others. I am convinced that *you should only lead people if you like people.*

Happy employees work better

Researchers at the University of Warwick in London wanted to study what happiness does to work performance. They invited a number of software developers into the lab and gave them all the same programming task, making it easy to gauge how productive they were. Before the volunteers started on the task, the researchers made some of them a little happier by either showing them a brief comedy video or feeding them chocolate. These "treated" subjects became 12% more productive on the task. One of the researchers, Dr. Daniel Sgroi, explained the results like this:

> *The driving force seems to be that happier workers use the time they have more effectively, increasing the pace at which they can work without sacrificing quality.*

His colleague, Dr. Eugenio Proto, said leaders should take these results seriously:

> *We have shown that happier subjects are more productive, the same pattern appears in four different experiments. This research will provide some guidance for management in all kinds of organizations, they should strive to make their workplaces emotionally healthy for their workforce.*

You may argue that 12% doesn't sound like much of a productivity increase, but remember that all they did was feed them chocolate or show them a funny video, creating a brief spike of positive emotions. Now, imagine the productivity increase from consistently loving what you do over a long period. There is a huge amount of research being conducted on how positive emotions affect our work performance, and so far we know that happy employees have a performance advantage in all of these areas:

- More productive
- More creative
- More helpful
- More energy
- Better at service
- More focused on quality
- Better team-players
- More open
- More likable
- More empathetic
- More resilient
- Sell more
- More optimistic
- More motivated
- More engaged
- Faster learners

Take a look at this list and consider which of these are most important for your team? Which three of these advantages are key to improving performance in your organization or team, with the kind of work your people do? It's worth noting that you get all of these effects when people experience positive emotions at work *right now* and when they're having a good day *today*—not when they're generally satisfied with their work situation.

Happy companies make more money

Working on a big Hollywood movie can certainly be stressful and tough, so when director JJ Abrams was filming "Star Wars: The Force Awakens" in 2015, he decided he wanted to create a happy, respectful atmosphere on set. Abrams realized that this would not just make for a nicer experience for everyone involved, it would also make people work harder and better on the movie. In a conversation with the legendary screenwriter Lawrence Kasdan, he said this:

> *When you respect each other, it's amazing what gets done.*
>
> *It sounds pollyannaish like it's all, you know, flowers and cookies, but it's not that at all—it's a lot of bleeping[III] hard work.*

The movie was a huge hit and set a world record by grossing $1 billion in just its first 12 days in theaters. Because happy employees do better work, happy companies make more money. Studies have found that happy companies have[70]:

- Higher sales.
- Higher customer loyalty.
- Higher growth.
- Higher stock prices.
- Higher profits.

One researcher concluded that[71]:

> *A large and growing body of research on positive organizational psychology demonstrates that not only is a cut-throat environment harmful to productivity over time, but that a positive environment will lead to dramatic benefits for employers, employees, and the bottom line.*

In addition to the fact that happy employees do better work, we also know that happy workplaces:

- Have much lower absenteeism.
- Have lower employee turnover.
- Spend less time and money recruiting new people.
- Attract the best talent.

All of this means that leaders are not making a choice between employee happiness and business results, sacrificing

---

III Of course, he didn't say "bleeping."

one to achieve the other. Instead, happy leaders realize that the two go hand in hand and that happy employees drive great results.

Søren Lockwood is the CEO of SEB Pension in Denmark, a financial organization employing 300 people. His job as leader of this workplace is to drive growth and profits, but he realized a few years ago that the best way to do it was to have happy employees and has since made happiness at work a top strategic priority. In 2015, he even won a national HR award, which is quite a rare event for a CEO.

He told me that he is always asked if he can prove that this focus on happiness creates business results and that he's a little frustrated with the question. His answer was:

> *What about all the leaders who focus on destroying happiness? Why don't they have to prove that it doesn't work?*

So, let me just point out that SEB Pension not only has happy employees, they also have excellent financial results and have the highest customer satisfaction ratings among all the pension companies in Denmark. All of this means that you're not choosing between employee happiness and business results. Bob Chapman of Barry-Wehmiller explained it like this:

> *There was an article in Inc. Magazine about Barry-Wehmiller with the headline "people over profits." But that's not true.*
>
> *If we don't create value, we won't exist as an organization. Because if you ignore the economic value, you will lose the company.*
>
> *Between people and profits, it's not one over the other. The two are in harmony.*

Happy leaders find a way to lead that doesn't sacrifice one for the other.

Who is responsible for employee happiness?

Who is responsible for making employees happy at work? Is

it their direct manager? Is it the top executives or the board? Or are employees responsible for their own happiness?

This is a crucial question that contains several dangerous traps. One trap is to say that "Employees are solely responsible for their own happiness at work. It doesn't matter what managers do, employees can always make themselves happy, or they can just quit." I've heard bad managers use this is an excuse to not care about their employees. Another trap is to lay the responsibility solely at the feet of the immediate manager and saying that "managers are responsible for making every employee happy at all times." That can't work because happiness is an internal emotional state that you can't create in others against their will. Here's how we see it:

- Top executives are responsible for designing organizational structures, values, and processes that promote happiness at work.
- Middle managers are responsible for creating a structure and culture in their team that makes it easy for employees to be happy at work.
- Employees have a responsibility to create happiness at work for themselves and their coworkers within the framework of the organization.

So, you, as a leader, are not responsible for making every single one of your people happy at work. Your job is to create conditions that promote happiness. Leaders can certainly do that. And some leaders do the opposite and create conditions that virtually guarantee misery and stress.

How do leaders make employees happier?

Now that we've established the business case for happiness, and seen that happy employees are happier, healthier, and more productive, and happy companies make more money, it's time to ask the most important question: How? What exactly can great leaders do to make their employees happier?

It's worth looking back to the chapter on Positive Psychology and see how we can apply those lessons. Here are five of the most important findings and how they can inform what leaders do to make their employee happier.

Because	Focus less on	Focus more on
Happiness is more about emotions than satisfaction	Salaries, bonuses, titles, and perks	Results and relationships
Appreciating the good things we have makes us happy	Pointing out and fixing problems	Pointing out and celebrating the good things in the workplace
Small actions make us happy	Big events like the annual office party or team building activities	Daily interactions
Positive surprises make us happy	Planned, recurring actions	Surprising, new actions
We get most happiness from making others happier	Doing things for employees	Helping employees do things for others, e.g. customers and co-workers

The most important point to remember is that *happiness is something we do*. If you want your employees to be happier, you have to do something to make that happen. No book can tell you what *you* should do, but the rest of this chapter offers some inspiring examples from many happy leaders that you can adapt to your leadership.

Give positive feedback

A 2015 study confirmed what we all know: Receiving positive

feedback makes us happier at work, less stressed, and more productive[72]. In the experiment, participants were given a series of tasks to solve as quickly as possible and just before they began, some of them received positive feedback. Specifically, they read an email from a friend or coworker that described a situation where they performed at their best—what the researchers called best-self activation.

The subjects who received this positive feedback ended up doing much better. In one test, participants had three minutes to complete one specific creative challenge, the classic Duncker Candle Stick Problem. 51% of those who had read emails prior to the task were able to successfully complete it while only 19% of those who did not receive "best-self activation" emails made it in time. The praised volunteers also reported feeling less stressed while solving the tasks and tests of their saliva showed less cortisol[IV] than the unpraised subjects.

The researchers summed up the results like this:

> *Best-self activation inspired improvements in people's emotions, resistance to disease, resilience to stress and burnout, creative problem solving, performance under pressure, and relationships with their employer.*

Why is positive feedback so effective? It's simple: Praise causes positive emotions, and as we know from research in positive psychology, positive emotions are good for us and improve performance.

Sadly, praise is rare in the workplace. In a 2015 study of unhappiness at work that my company conducted, "A lack of praise and recognition" was one of the major causes of bad days at work. 37% of participants mentioned it as something that made them unhappy at work[73].

Clearly many workplaces have no tradition of positive feedback. Many managers, in particular, have developed a notion that praise is trivial or ineffective—they're completely wrong, of course. I've even heard managers argue that "we shouldn't praise employees—they're just doing their jobs." How incredibly narrow-minded. Some workplaces even have a strong culture of negative feedback, so that good performance is

---

IV High levels of cortisol can be a sign of stress.

met with silence, but the slightest mistake is punished harshly.

Not only does the current absence of praise in the workplace make it harder to praise people, it might even mean that any praise you start giving is initially met with scorn or suspicion. Stick with it. Over time, people will come to realize that the praise is genuine and not just an attempt to butter them up for something else.

It's clear that praise at work is important because it shows people that they do good work, make a difference, and get *results*. This gives us a feeling of pride that makes us very happy at work. Praise also motivates us for future tasks. But there is more to positive feedback; it's also about strengthening *relationships* in the workplace. When you praise someone else, it shows that you actually pay attention to them, value them, and are able to see their good work and positive qualities.

The German sociologist Axel Honneth has suggested that recognition is foundational for our relationships to others and even to ourselves[74]:

> *In order to develop a practical identity, persons fundamentally depend on the feedback of other subjects (and of society as a whole). Those who fail to experience adequate recognition, i.e., those who are depicted by the surrounding others or the societal norms and values in a one-sided or negative way, will find it much harder to embrace themselves and their projects as valuable. Misrecognition thereby hinders or destroys persons' successful relationship to their selves.*

One of our most fundamental psychological needs is for others to see and recognize the good in us, and Honneth argues that how others see us is one of the major factors that shape our identity. People who are never seen, or only seen for the bad they do, are much less happy and have a much higher risk of developing mental problems over time.

Fortunately, there are many companies and leaders who do get it. One example is Richard Branson of Virgin who has a tremendous focus on celebrating and praising his people. He wrote that:

I have always believed that the way you treat your employees is the way they will treat your customers, and that people flourish if they're praised.

So, praise your employees. It's one of the most effective ways to make a workplace happier and more productive. Positive feedback takes no time and costs no money. But it does require two things from you:

1. You see the good work your people do and the good qualities your people have
2. You tell them about it

Could you become the kind of leader who is really good at seeing the good in your people *and* telling them about it? When you praise your employees, you don't have to make a big production out of it. You could:

- Simply go up to an employee and tell them the positive feedback.
- Send praise in an email.
- Write positive feedback on a post-it note and stick it on their desk.
- Say "thank you" in person or in emails.
- Praise someone in a meeting in front of their coworkers.

Think about the recipient and choose a form of praise they will enjoy. It's also worth remembering that good praise is:

- Genuine—only praise people if you mean it.
- Meaningful—praise people for something that is worth praising and not for trivial things; and.
- Specific—tell them what was good.

Finally, you don't have to wait for someone to do stellar, fantastic, amazing work before you praise them. You can praise different aspects of your employees:

- What they do—their work or their results. "Good job getting that new client."
- Their effort—how hard and determined they work. "I really admire how hard you've been working on getting new clients."

- Their personality—the good personal qualities you see in them. "You're such an engaging person, our prospective new clients really enjoy meeting you."

Make it a daily challenge to give at least one employee positive feedback of some kind. This can help develop a habit around it and get to the point where it's something you do naturally. Jack Mitchell, the owner of two very successful clothing stores in New England and author of the excellent book "Hug your People," had a very practical way to remind himself to give positive feedback: Every morning he'd put 10 coins in his left trouser pocket. Every time he praised an employee, he'd move one coin to the right pocket, and he wouldn't go home from work before all the coins were in the other pocket.

You can also get your employees to praise each other, so all positive feedback doesn't have to flow from the top. At one IKEA warehouse we worked with, leadership created a "Praise Wall" where employees could pin notes of praise for their coworkers, for everyone to see. One senior surgeon at a hospital filled a cupboard in his office with chocolate and told his entire staff that they were always welcome to come in and take some chocolate to give to a coworker that they wanted to praise.

Listen to your people

Benjamin Zander, the happy conductor we met previously, invites his musicians to share their problems and disagreements:

> *I give every member of the orchestra a voice at every rehearsal, in the form of a sheet of paper on which they can write anything that they want about the experience that is working or not working. And without any holds barred. If something is not working in the music or something's not working in my conducting, they're completely free to say so.*
>
> *They sign their name so that we can continue the conversation, and that is a very, very powerful tool*

because it means that even if you're sitting in the seventeenth chair and are completely anonymous, you have a say.

One of my second violinists does this frequently. He'll send me a three-page email, single-spaced, about this tempo wasn't right, and you made the crescendo too early and all these instructions, all of which I take completely seriously. He's very thoughtful. And the fact that he's in the second violins doesn't mean that he's any less valuable than the first trumpet.

Happy leaders listen to their people and act on what they hear. And if your people tell you you've made a mistake, go ahead and apologize. Ben does it all the time:

I apologized to the Israel Philharmonic for a mistake I made and one of the players told me, "I don't think I ever heard a conductor apologize for their frequent mistakes in the last 25 years."

There really is no substitute for listening to your people. Talk to them individually and in groups. Invite their honest opinion. Then act on what you hear. The coolest way I've seen this being done is at a marketing agency, Quirk, based in Cape Town, Johannesburg and the UK.

They created a process that lets anyone in the company raise issues, gather support for them and get them implemented quickly. When I visited their Cape Town HQ, I had a chance to see it for myself, and I think every workplace that wants to give their employees a voice should do something similar.

If an employee has a suggestion or sees a problem, the first step is to post it to a board that hangs in a prominent spot in the office. The next step is to get 12 coworkers (10% of the staff) to sign on. If people like an idea, they show their support in a very low-tech way: they put a sticker on it.

If an idea gets the necessary support, the person behind it writes a one-page proposal, which is then submitted to Quirk's EXCO, which is basically their top leadership team. This group meets every other week, and the suggestion goes on the agenda for the next meeting, ensuring a fast response. If they approve it, the idea goes ahead immediately. Of course, the leadership group can turn the idea down, but if they do, they must carefully and in great detail explain why they don't think it can be done. They can't just say "No" or "Maybe later." This process is fast, easy, and transparent and means that any employee can raise any idea or concern and quickly get a response.

Menlo Innovations, an IT company in Ann Arbor, Michigan, also encourages bad news and complaints from their employees. I asked Rich Sheridan, their co-founder and Chief Storyteller, what his most important job as a leader is. He immediately replied:

Pumping fear out of the room.

His main role is to create clarity and take away the fears and frustrations that make people unhappy at work. To this end, they train leaders at Menlo to always listen to complaints and bad news from employees with a smile and respond with "thank you for telling me that."

Meaning and purpose

Henrik Egeskov is a department head at The Patient Compensation Association, a government agency that decides compensation claims for patients injured in connection to treatment provided by the Danish Health Service. His team of legal and medical experts are incredibly busy judging claims by patients and determining whether they're eligible for compensation and, if so, how much. In that situation, it's easy to get bogged down in just working on the next case and the next one after that and forget that you're actually making a difference in people's lives.

So, he asked each of his employees to guess how much money his team had paid out in compensation in the last six months and email him their best guess. He accessed their systems and found that the amount was DKK 51,604,788 (around $8 million). For the next department meeting, he baked a cake and wrote "51,604,788 - great work" on the icing. This was a great chance for the team to remind themselves that their work is ultimately helping real people and that they make many patients happier by getting them the compensation they're entitled to. He told me the message (and the cake) were received very positively.

In most workplaces, we have a pretty clear picture of *what* we do, but sometimes we become so focused on the next task, the next meeting, the next email, or the next phone call that we forget *why* we're doing it. There is very little happiness in just completing one task after another if we have no idea why those tasks matter. On the other hand, when employees know that their work makes a positive difference for someone, work is much more meaningful, and they have a much stronger feeling of results.

Some jobs offer this implicitly. Nurses in a hospital can see the patients get better. Teachers can see students pick up new knowledge. If you design solar cells, you are helping combat climate change. Many public-sector workplaces, in general, have the advantage that what they do is not for profit but in direct service of the public, and therefore more directly meaningful, which means that government workplaces are in an excellent position to be happy workplaces. This actually gives them a competitive edge compared to private workplaces that often focus more on profits than on making a positive difference.

Conflict can arise when leaders measure employees on factors that are not meaningful to them. Most nurses are not motivated by tasks, deadlines, and budgets but by being able to heal people. Most teachers are not driven by schedules, plans, and to do lists but by improving students' lives.

I worked with one very financially successful insurance company that was seeing a sharp rise in employee stress and unhappiness. One problem was that they increasingly measured their customer service employees on factors like "number of calls handled," frustrating the employees, who mostly found meaning in doing their jobs well and helping the customers.

It's important to take a pause once in a while from *what* we do at work and remind ourselves *why* we do it. If you can't immediately see how the work your organization or team does is meaningful, ask some of these questions: "Who are we making happier? Who are we helping? Whose lives are better, easier, safer, or healthier because of the work we do?" The answer can be external (e.g., customers) or internal (e.g., co-workers or others teams), but if you can't honestly say that the work your team and organization does is helping anyone in any way, then that work is essentially meaningless and it's hard to see how anyone could possibly be happy doing it.

In the next two chapters, we're going to look specifically at ways to create more happiness for customers and the wider community, and one advantage of also focusing on these groups is that making others happier gives work purpose and meaning. When you, as a leader, know that your leadership not only benefits yourself and your people, but even makes your customers and the community happier, work becomes infused with meaning and purpose.

I worked with a big multinational company, which makes medical devices, to make two of their factories happier workplaces. Some of the production processes involve a lot of manual labor, where employees are putting together the products by hand, in this case, urine drainage bags and catheters used by people who can no longer control their bladders. They'd had some problems with the quality of the finished products, which were often assembled incorrectly, causing problems for the users.

They got the idea to bring in two of their customers one day to talk to the employees over lunch. These were people in wheelchairs who talked about what life is like as a disabled person, how they depended on the products the company makes, and what happens when the products are faulty—for instance, if a urine bag leaks. This clearly showed the employees that their work matters and makes a positive difference for someone who really needs it. Now they knew not just *what* they were doing, but *why* they were doing it. The employees became happier at work and error rates in the finished products dropped.

George Bernard Shaw said it best:

> *This is the true joy in life, the being used for a purpose recognized by yourself as a mighty one; the being thoroughly worn out before you are thrown on the*

scrap heap; the being a force of Nature instead of a feverish selfish little clod of ailments and grievances complaining that the world will not devote itself to making you happy.

Give your people freedom

When David Marquet took command of the nuclear submarine USS Santa Fe, he knew he needed to make significant changes. It had the worst performance record of all American nuclear submarines, was never ready for its missions on time, and was basically the laughing stock of the US Navy.

The crew was miserable too. Out of 135 sailors, only three had chosen to reenlist and stay on the boat the year before. In fact, the reason David became the captain was that the previous captain had suddenly quit. David came in with a plan to improve the results on the submarine and thereby make its crew happier. But he told me that he found that he had to do it the other way around: Make the submarine a happy workplace and results would follow.

David's main change was that he stopped giving orders and instead focused on creating the right vision and atmosphere, making sure that every single sailor knew what the submarine's current goals were and was free to think for themselves in how to achieve those goals. As he told me:

Instead of letting information flow to the people with decision power, we gave decision power to the people who had the information.

It worked, and the USS Santa Fe became the Navy's best performing submarine. He's shared the story in his extraordinary book "Turn the Ship Around," which I highly recommend. Here's how he sums up his message:

Bad leaders give bad orders.

Good leaders give good orders.

Great leaders give no orders.

Countless studies show that when employees have freedom

and autonomy at work, they are happier and more engaged.

> Peer1 hosting in Southampton in the UK hosts big websites for corporate clients who are highly invested in their websites being available at all times. The occasional downtime is limited but cannot be avoided. Their CEO at the time, Dominic Monkhouse, told me that they used to have a policy that their front-line supporters could give customers a refund in the case of service interruptions but only up to a certain amount. Above that amount, the employee had to get approval from a manager, which took time and resources.
>
> So, Dominic decided to change that policy and give the supporters a free hand in deciding how big of a refund to grant customers. This had three results:
>
> 1. Employees were happier because they felt empowered and trusted.
> 2. Customers were happier because they got their refunds faster now that managers didn't have to be involved.
> 3. The company ended up refunding *less* money to customers because the supporters knew every detail of the case and could better gauge a fair compensation, whereas managers tended to approve anything.

Some companies go the other way and try to have rules and policies for everything. Here is the bereavement policy from a US university that states how much time employees get off in case of a death in the family:

> *Staff members shall, upon request, be granted up to three (3) days annually of bereavement leave for the death of a parent, spouse, child, brother or sister, grandparents [sic], grandparents-in-law, grandchild, son or daughter-in-law, mother-in-law, father-in-law, brother-in-law, sister-in-law, stepchildren, children-in-law, aunts, uncles, nieces, nephews, and first and second cousins. Other relationships are excluded unless there is a guardian relationship. Such leave is non-accumulative, and the total amount of bereavement leave will not exceed three days within any fiscal year. If additional days of absences are*

necessary, employees may request sick or annual leave, after providing an explanation of extenuating circumstances.

Got that? How utterly pedantic and inhumane. Contrast that with Middelfart Savings Bank. They have 300 employees and are based in a Danish town called Middelfart, which in Danish simply means "middle of the way." Go ahead and giggle at the name, if you like—the town's Wikipedia page does mention that "the name is considered humorous to English speakers," and it certainly gets a laugh every time I mention them in front of an English-speaking audience. Regardless of the name, the company is an amazing workplace and has taken first place in the Danish Great Place to Work Survey four times. In 2017, they came in third in Europe.

The bank's 2017 Culture Profile describes their policy in the event of a death in the family, essentially boiling it down to "Talk to us, and we'll figure out how much time you need off." Some employees may need to take a longer leave of absence to recover, whereas others might actually prefer to get back to work sooner because doing their jobs and being with their coworkers helps them.

Middelfart Savings Bank has taken that approach as far as they can and essentially eliminated all rules and bureaucracy. There is no upper limit on what size loans individual employees can approve for clients, instead, they're expected to exercise their good judgment. There are no dress codes because employees are trusted to dress appropriately. I've always felt that dress codes are dumb and that if you have to tell your employees how to dress, you have bigger problems. The unofficial dress code at Google is simply "You must wear clothes."

Middelfart bank's CFO told me that one of the branch managers called him because he was throwing a party for his employees, and wanted to know "What's my budget per employee for an internal party?" The CFO quickly replied "How should I know," and hung up on him. His point was that the bank has no rules for this kind of thing—instead trusting the managers' judgment—but also that if you give people a budget limit, they tend to go to that limit. In this case, the branch manager ended up having the party at his house and cooking for his staff himself, which was not only cheaper but also much more personal and memorable than going to a fancy restaurant.

> NRI Distribution in Canada is a logistics company that distributes goods for big brands like Volcom, Marmot, and Skullcandy. They used to have something called *the 15-centimeter rule*. Their first location in Canada is close to some excellent ski resorts, so the rule was simply this: If there is more than 15 centimeters of fresh snow in the mountains, you can take off from work and go skiing or snowboarding.
>
> Their CFO and co-founder, Bruce Churchill, told me that now that the company has grown and added new locations and a more diverse staff, the policy has evolved into a flexible work environment:
>
> "When people look to take time off or adjust their work schedule, we do whatever we can to accommodate. We still have people who ask to take a morning or a day off to hit the slopes but that also goes for people wanting to see their kids in a school play, taking time to visit with friends or family from out of town in on a surprise visit, or any other event that may be important to our people.
>
> There are times when we simply can't say yes as the need is too great, but when that happens, people accept it because they know we always do everything we can to accommodate them so "no" means there's a real need."
>
> The rule evolved, but the philosophy is the same. They value their employees and want to give them the chance to enjoy the fresh powder or a child's school play while it's there, and their employees enjoy not only the privilege but also the trust it demonstrates in them.

Let people do their jobs—don't put endless rules, regulations, and bureaucracy in their way. As much as possible, set your people free to work when they want, where they want, on what they want, with whom they want, in the way they want. They will be happier and much more productive than if you're there micromanaging them every step of the way.

Hire for happiness

It's safe to say that many leaders primarily try to hire applicants with the best skills and previous work experience. This can backfire big time, as Next Jump's CEO, Charlie Kim, told me:

> *We followed a common practice used by the biggest tech companies in the world: to hire brilliant and driven people. After two years of heavily investing in this hiring process, concentrating our efforts at the top engineering schools on the east coast, we found ourselves with a small army of brilliant jerks.*
>
> *The culture was toxic. Racial tension, blaming others, total disregard for other people's opinions and total protection of one's own ideas and work products. We did a rapid evaluation of all the people we would want to work with vs. those we didn't, and, in one day, we fired half our engineers.*

If you want to create a happy workplace, you can't hire miserable people. They will come in and make their coworkers equally miserable through their actions, attitudes, and *emotional contagion*. Instead, hire for happiness. The incredibly successful British café chain Pret A Manger do this, saying:

> *You can't hire someone who can make sandwiches and teach them to be happy. So we hire happy people and teach them to make sandwiches.*

How do you know if a potential hire is happy? If you ask them directly if they are happy, they can't really say anything but "Yeah, sure, I guess..." Instead, ask them questions about specific previous positive work experiences, such as:

- Who's the best co-worker you ever had? What did you like about that person?
- Tell me about the best manager you've worked for. What did you like about him/her?
- What is the most fun project you've ever worked on?
- What's been one of your proudest moments at work?

Note that the questions are about *specific* experiences. Don't ask "What makes a good boss in your opinion?" Ask specifically about the best boss they've worked for previously and what made that boss good. Happy people generally have an easier time remembering previous positive experiences and will have ready answers to questions like this. Furthermore, questions like this will make the interview a more pleasant experience and give you a clear picture of what circumstances this applicant thrives well in.

It's not necessarily about hiring people who are already happy. Rather, the point is to take great care in hiring someone who will be happy in that job, i.e., have great results and great relationships. It's a hallmark of happy workplaces that they hire very, very carefully. Valve, a software company in Seattle, says it most clearly in their employee handbook[75]:

> *Hiring well is the most important thing in the universe.*
>
> *Everything else in our world is subordinate to finding great people and keeping the bar high.*

The Dutch football[V] club, Ajax Amsterdam, has a highly successful youth academy where they recruit and train the potential football stars of the future. But how do you know who's got it? How can you tell if this or that 10-year old kid will grow up to be a football legend? Interestingly, the biggest talents are not necessarily the ones who score the most goals. One of their talent spotters, Roland de Jong, said[76]:

> *I am never looking for a result—for example, which boy is scoring the most goals or even who is running the fastest. That may be because of their size and stage of development. I want to notice how a boy runs. Is he on his forefeet, running lightly? Does he have creativity with the ball? Does it seem that he is really loving the game? I think these things are good at predicting how he'll be when he is older.*

V That's "soccer" to all US readers.

This is even more important when hiring managers. Rosenbluth International, a US corporate travel agency with 6,000 employees, had decided to make their employees' happiness the company's top priority. Their CEO, Hal Rosenbluth, wrote an excellent book called "The Customer Comes Second: Put Your People First and Watch'em Kick Butt", and this story from his book shows how careful they were about hiring for management positions:

> Rosenbluth was once about to hire an executive with all the right skills, the right personality, and the perfect CV. His interviews went swimmingly, and he said all the right things, but something about him still made Rosenbluth nervous, though he couldn't put his finger on just what it was. His solution was brilliant: He invited the applicant to join a company softball game, and here he showed his true colors. He was competitive to the point of being manic. He abused and yelled at both the opponents and his own team. He cursed the referees and kicked up dirt like a major league player. And he did not get the job.

Stop bad employee behavior

> One of our clients, a huge insurance company, had a team of 50 claims handlers who were getting more and more unhappy at work. There were many factors in play, but one reason was that one of their most senior employees had become incredibly negative at work. She would complain about everything and everybody, she would shoot down all new ideas, and she was almost always irritable and snappy with her coworkers. She also had this habit where she would end most phone calls by slamming down the receiver, staring at the phone and sneering "Idiot."
>
> Even though she was amazing at her job and knew all the systems and processes inside out, the leader of this team realized that this behavior could not go on. So, he prepared thoroughly and then called her in for a meeting in which he clearly laid out the situation as he saw it. He gave examples of her negative behavior, and how it affected him and the coworkers, making them feel anxious, de-energized and frustrated. He also made it clear that she either had to

change her behavior or she would be fired. He then gave her the rest of the day off to think about it.

The next day she came back to work and in a meeting with the manager told him that she'd thought about it and actually agreed that her behavior had become increasingly negative. She told him that that wasn't the person she wanted to be and asked for his help to change. Over the next few months she gradually learned to behave in a very different way, and after three months, she stood up at a staff meeting and apologized to her co-workers for her behavior and thanked the manager for helping her realize that she needed to change. She became happier, her co-workers became happier, and the team achieved better results than ever.

Certain employee behaviors can be a disaster for the whole team, including:

- Bullying
- Rude/disrespectful behavior
- Rumors/gossip
- Lying/cheating
- Constant complaining

Bullying in the workplace, in particular, can be psychologically disastrous[77]. Fortunately, it's quite rare, but when it does happen it can ruin the target's life, and it must be stopped *immediately*.

If you see any of this go on in your team, you have to address it and stop it. This is hard. If the quality of an employee's work is not high enough, that's a lot easier to address because we're not criticizing the person directly, we're criticizing their work. But when the problem lies with the employees' personal behavior at work, it hits a lot harder to home and can be much more difficult to address.

That's why you must prepare well as the manager in the story above did. The communication process called Non-Violent Communication developed by Marshall Rosenberg[78] can be a great framework for these difficult conversations, and is broken down into the following four steps:

1. Observation: What behavior has that person been

engaged in? "I've seen you be rude to a co-worker three times this month when work gets busy. You coworkers tell me that it's happened several times more."

2. Feelings: How does this make you and others feel? "It makes me feel like you disrespect your coworkers. It makes them sad and fearful. One of them was in tears after what you said."
3. Needs: What do you need and value? "We need to treat each other with respect. I value when people treat each other kindly and with understanding, especially in stressful situations."
4. Request: What is your request for a specific action, free of demand? "I suggest that you apologize to the people in question and that we think about ways I can help you change that pattern of behavior."

And if the employee can't stop the negative behavior, it may be necessary to fire that person. Rosenbluth International, the corporate travel agency, faced this very dilemma. As an organization, they had decided to put their people first and make their employees' happiness the company's top priority. But, if you've put your people first, how can you fire anyone?

CEO Hal Rosenbluth did not see this dilemma. To him, putting your people first entails a responsibility to fire people who don't fit in. Employees shouldn't be fired at the first sign of trouble–training, coaching, guidance, or a new position inside the company could help to motivate them. However, when these things don't work, a commitment to your employees' happiness means that you have to fire employees that don't fit in. Allowing an employee to stay in a job that doesn't make them happy is not only bad for the employee, but for everyone around that person because of emotional contagion.

Build relationships with your employees

I received this message from a reader of my first book:

> I once worked for a bank in Germany—two locations in which you would not normally expect "personal affection."
>
> The team was large, about 40 people working in one open space office. It surprised me a lot that every morning,

> whoever arrived, walked through the whole office and greeted everybody with a handshake and some personal words. It did not matter if the team members came, the bosses from higher up or anybody from another department. It was known everywhere that here you greet everybody personally.
>
> For the first week, I found that very strange and a bit intimidating. Also, it cost a lot of time all in all. Yet, afterward, I really enjoyed it. It gave everybody the chance to get to know their colleagues a bit better, to hear what they are off to, or to realize that somebody is not in or just returned from a trip or vacation. There was no need to e-mail weekly lists on who is out when. We just knew it.
>
> By the way, when I moved on to another job, I sort of missed it.

Employees should have no doubt that their immediate leader sees them, knows them, and genuinely cares about their performance and happiness. In short, they should have a great working relationship with their leader, and one incredibly simple way to achieve that is for the leader to greet employees in the morning. Try it yourself: Make it a habit to go around to each of your employees in the morning and say a friendly, cheerful "good morning." It lets your people know that you see them and care about them.

Every interaction you have with your employees—meetings, emails, phone calls, coffee breaks, lunch breaks, passing each other in the halls—is a chance to build relationships and happy leaders do this every chance they get.

A few years ago, The Danish Association of Managers and Executives published a study showing that 60% of Danish managers felt they have too little time for their work because they spend too much time on their employees. Nonsense! As a manager, your employees are your job. Your very first priority is to keep them happy and productive. Of course, all managers have other things to do as well, but if you put your own assignments above those of your immediate subordinates, the result will be an increase in one person's efficiency (yours) at the expense of that of 10 to 20 others (depending on how many you are responsible for). If you're not 10 to 20 times more productive than them, then that's a really bad trade. Building good relationships means that you need to have time for your people every single day.

Here's a very simple way to do it: Every day, take five minutes to talk to one of your employees with no other agenda. Just go up and ask how they are and what's going on. If it's Monday, ask about their weekend. If they just came back from vacation, ask how it was. Each day, talk to someone else and then back to the first person.

Leaders with strong relationship skills probably do something like this already and don't need to give it any additional structure. Results-oriented leaders, however, tend to get caught up in the number and spreadsheets, and every interaction they have with their people is about the work. This is a great way for those leaders to give these interpersonal touch points some structure and form.

If you're a very results-driven person, I would even suggest creating a spreadsheet with all your employees' names in one column and the date you last took five minutes with that person in the second column. That makes it easy to see who you haven't connected with for a while. You can put "Take 5" in your calendar every day—say from 11.00 to 11.05—to remind yourself to do it, until it becomes a habit.

Top executives of large companies can't form meaningful relationships with every single person in the organization, but they can still make an effort to connect. After one of my speeches in Istanbul, I met a top executive of a huge Turkish organization with thousands of employees who has had a wonderful tradition for the last many years: Every month he has lunch with ten randomly picked employees. These ten employees not only get a nice lunch—over the course of a couple of hours get to ask any question they want and air any concerns or complaints. They also get a chance to meet him in an informal setting and get a sense of who he is as a person, and he gets direct feedback on how his employees are doing.

All of this aims to create a workplace where people like each other, trust each other, and work well together. The Canadian leadership academic and author Henry Mintzberg puts it like this:

Corporations are social institutions, which function best when committed human beings (not human "resources") collaborate in relationships based on trust and respect. Destroy this and the whole institution of business collapses.

Random acts of workplace kindness

Two sales managers at one of our clients wanted to do something special for their employees, so one Monday morning they got to work early and greeted every single of their 80 people as they arrived for work with a cheerful good morning and a breakfast plate to take up to their desks. A few months later as Christmas was approaching, they put on Christmas elf hats and went around the whole office serving sweets to everyone.

A random act of workplace kindness is a small act you do for one or more employees that they don't know is coming and it can be surprisingly effective for two reasons. First, as we saw in the section on the neuroscience of happiness on page 35, positive surprises make people happier than things they know about in advance. Secondly, when you do nice things for others, it shows that you care and strengthens relationships.

And it can be really small things. Try some of these:

- Next time you're getting yourself a coffee, bring an extra for someone who didn't ask for it.
- Go around your team handing out candy.
- Leave a chocolate bar on someone's desk anonymously.

You can also encourage your people to do nice things for each other—as we've seen previously, making others happier makes us happier.

Don't just reward results—celebrate results

It's probably not every day that you see your CEO playing air guitar. If it is, I want to meet your CEO. But the employees of a Danish IT company had that pleasure a few years ago. All employees were asked to come to the cafeteria for an important announcement. It turned out their company had just won two huge new clients for their software, but instead of just announcing this to polite applause, they put on rock music and the CEO played air guitar.

Can't you just pay your employees to get better results? Sadly, no. Research consistently shows that promising people a bonus to achieve better results makes people perform *worse*. Dan Ariely, Professor of Psychology and Behavioral Economics at Duke University, tried this in the real world. He worked with a semiconductor factory in Israel, an ideal test case because here they could measure productivity directly by seeing how many units were produced by each employee each day.

Employees were divided into four different groups:

1. Some were promised a cash bonus (about $30) if they reached a certain production goal that day
2. Some were promised a free pizza if they reached the same goal
3. Some got a message from their boss thanking them if they reached the goal
4. The control group who worked as usual

The experiment very clearly showed the limitations of bonuses. The workers in group 1 increased productivity that day by 4.9%, but the next day, when a cash bonus was no longer offered, their output *fell* by 13.2%. Over the whole week, this group produced 6.5% *less* than the control group. On the other hand, pizza and notes of gratitude both led to an increase in productivity on the day itself of 6.5% which carried over and also increased production over the next few days. The American sociologist Alfie Kohn sums up the research into rewards like this:

> *One of the most thoroughly replicated findings in the field of social psychology states, the more you reward people for doing something, the more they tend to lose interest in whatever they had to do to get the reward.*

The science is clear: Performance rewards *reduce performance* because they make employees focus more on the reward than on the work, they narrow people's thinking and make them less creative and because rewards are an extrinsic motivator that kills employees' engagement in the work itself, i.e., their intrinsic motivation.

So, happy leaders focus more on *celebrating performance* and less on rewarding performance. Richard Branson does this during the annual Virgin Star of the Year Award where outstanding employees from his companies all over the world are celebrated for making Virgin a successful and fun workplace. The winners receive no cash award but they are celebrated in front of their peers, and they get a star named after them.

Celebrate mistakes

If you're ever in Waterbury, Vermont, you should definitely visit Ben and Jerry's for a tour of their HQ to get an insight into how they make their amazing ice cream and the values that guide them. And while you're there, also check out their *flavor graveyard*[79]. Where many companies hide their fiascos, Ben and Jerry's proudly display their failed flavors by giving each of them a headstone and an accompanying verse.

In some workplaces, employees who do good work go unrecognized, but anyone who makes a mistake is immediately and harshly punished. This is dumb. When employees can openly admit to screwing up without fear of reprisals, they're more likely to fess up and learn from their mistakes. And that's why leaders should help employees celebrate mistakes.

Conductor Ben Zander teaches his musicians a fantastic way to do that:

> *The great fear of musicians is that they will make a mistake. They live in that kind of fear. What I say to my musicians and to my students is that whenever you make a mistake, you throw up your arms and with a smile say, "How fascinating!"*
>
> *I've been teaching this to people all around the corporate world who are now going, "How fascinating," when something goes wrong. The point about that is the hands go up, the face goes up, the body is lightened, and you have a chance to say, "How fascinating. What went wrong? What did I do? What can I do right the next time so I can avoid it again?" That puts you in a state of inquiry and learning.*
>
> *I want to make people feel comfortable about making mistakes, at peace with it. And I never get upset if somebody makes a mistake.*

Just to be clear, we're not celebrating the mistake itself. We're really celebrating that

1. We have the courage to try new things. When we do that, occasionally we will fail.
2. We have the courage to admit our mistakes and learn from them.

Those two things are worth celebrating. And it is extra important when you as the leader make a mistake. Instead of hiding it, celebrate it with your team.

The American management thinker Peter Drucker provocatively suggested that businesses should find all the employees who never make mistakes and fire them because employees who never make mistakes never do anything interesting. Admitting that mistakes happen and celebrating them when they do makes mistakes less likely. Menlo

Innovations even has a big banner hanging in their office that proudly says:

Make mistakes faster.

The prolific inventor James Dyson says this:

I made 5127 prototypes of my vacuum before I got it right. There were 5126 failures. But I learned from each one. That's how I came up with a solution. So I don't mind failure. I've always thought that schoolchildren should be marked by the number of failures they've had. The child who tries strange things and experiences lots of failures to get there is probably more creative...

We're taught to do things the right way. But if you want to discover something that other people haven't, you need to do things the wrong way. Initiate a failure by doing something that's very silly, unthinkable, naughty, dangerous. Watching why that fails can take you on a completely different path. It's exciting, actually.

So, my challenge to you is to start celebrating your failures. Next time you or someone on your team messes up, admit it, celebrate it, and learn from it. Tackle the mistake with humor and openness rather than with fear and shame.

Happy employees come first

We will end this chapter with the clearest expression of this philosophy that employee happiness must be a central strategic priority. Here's how Bob Chapman sees it:

At Barry-Wehmiller, our primary purpose is crystal clear to us: We're in business so that all our team members can have meaningful and fulfilling lives.

We do everything we can to create an environment in which our people can realize their gifts, apply and develop their talents, and feel a genuine sense of fulfillment for their contributions. In other words,

> *Barry-Wehmiller is in business to improve lives.*
>
> *We do that through the building of capital equipment and offering engineering consulting. But that's our what, not our why. It simply provides the vehicle, the economic engine through which we can enrich the lives of our team members.*

Chapman has fundamentally reimagined the fundamental nature of leadership and business. Instead of using people to achieve business goals, he uses business to achieve people goals. And interestingly, this ultimately leads to better business performance.

This chapter in tweets

- This strategy maximizes happiness AND profits: Employees come first, customers come second, the bottom line comes third.
- Leaders should forget about job satisfaction and make their employees happy.
- It's important for leaders to realize that happiness at work is not just for some job types or some employees. ANYONE can be happy at work.
- Raises, promotions, and perks don't make us happy at work. Results and relationships do, i.e., doing great work together with great people.
- The leader of the future is awesome at forming relationships with employees and customers alike.
- When leaders focus too much on results, it harms results!
- You can't lead people if you don't like people.
- Happiness at work is something we do, and there are many simple, effective ways for leaders to make their employees happier.
- You can't lead people if you don't like people.
- Happiness is the ultimate productivity booster. Happy employees are more motivated, more creative, more productive, and less sick.

- Happy companies make more money. Leaders who don't focus on happiness are hurting the bottom line.
- While leaders are not responsible for everyone being happy at all times, they are responsible for creating a structure and culture within which it's easy for employees to be happy.
- Many managers have a notion that praise is trivial or ineffective—they're completely wrong. Praise makes us happier and more effective.
- Happy leaders listen to their people and act on what they hear.
- It's important to take a break once in a while from what we do at work and remind ourselves why we do it.
- Give your employees freedom. "Bad leaders give bad orders. Good leaders give good orders. Great leaders give no orders."" - L. David Marquet
- Good leaders let people do their jobs and don't put endless rules, regulations, and bureaucracy in their way.
- If you want to create a happy workplace, you can't hire miserable people. Hire for happiness.
- Behaviors like bullying, gossiping, cheating, or constant complaining can be a disaster for a team. Leaders must stop them fast.
- Employees should have no doubt that their immediate leader sees them, knows them, and genuinely cares about their performance and happiness.
- Don't just reward results—celebrate results.
- The only people who never make mistakes are the ones who never do anything new. Encourage employees to celebrate their mistakes at work.

Happiness for customers

Complete this sentence: "When it rains, the price of umbrellas should go __."

If you guessed "up" you'd be right in most places. But at IKEA stores, you'd be wrong. Here's how they price their umbrellas depending on the weather:

- On sunny days umbrellas cost $4.99
- On rainy days they cost $2.50

Yes, on rainy days, umbrellas are cheaper at IKEA. What a nice way to make customers happy.

Without customers, there is no business, and most leaders are keenly aware of this. Customers are the very reason the organization exists in the first place. Realizing this, many leaders choose to measure and attempt to maximize *customer satisfaction*. As long as we offer the right products/services at the right price point and terms and keep our promises, the customer will be satisfied, and all will be good, right?

But what if you could go beyond that? What if you treat your customers in a way that not only makes them satisfied with your company's offerings but which makes their lives easier, safer, healthier, richer, more meaningful, more fun, or better in some other way? Not only do you get the joy of knowing that you're making their lives better, but it's also good for your business because happy customers are more likely to do the following:

- Return and buy more
- Recommend your products to others
- Forgive and forget if you make a mistake or can't keep a promise
- Stay customers even if someone is offering a competing product at a lower price

It's about making the mind shift from the rational concept of *customer satisfaction* to the more emotional *customer happiness*.

Customer satisfaction	**Customer happiness**
Deliver the right products/services at the right price	Make the customers' lives better
More rational	More emotional
Keep our promises	Surprise the customer
Results focus	Focus on long-term relationships
Transactional	Personal

How do we do that? One hugely important way is to have happy employees as we covered in the previous chapter. Happy employees care more about others, give better customer service, and have a natural desire to make others happy. Emotional contagion also comes into play, and happy employees make the customers happier simply by being genuinely happy themselves[80].

In the previous chapter, we also saw that the two main things that make employees happy at work are results and relationships, that these two represent our deepest psychological needs and are built into us on a biological level. This makes them equally useful for thinking about how to make customers happy. Let's look at some ways to make the customers happier.

Make your customer awesome

Why is it that the advertising brochure for a product is usually beautifully designed in full color on glossy paper, while the manual for the same product is often in black and white and printed on cheap flimsy paper? It's because many companies' main goal is to get you to buy their product, but once you own it, you're on your own. In her book "Badass: Making Users Awesome," Kathy Sierra argues that companies should change that approach and focus much more on teaching their customers to use their products:

> *The more you learn, the better you are at something. The better you are, the more engaging it is. If you can help people have more of that feeling, they won't talk about how good you are—they'll talk about how much they kick ass.*

This is a critical mind shift from "Focus on how awesome your product/service is" to "Focus on how awesome your customer is when they use your product/service." It doesn't matter how good your *product* is if it doesn't make the *customer* good. If you can help your customers become better at something, it gives them better results, which makes them happier.

WD-40 Company makes a lubricant with some amazing features, but their focus is not on how great their product is; It's on all the great things customers do with that product. In fact, their company purpose says nothing at all about their products:

> *We create positive lasting memories by solving problems in workshops, factories and homes around the world.*

A prominent section on their website showcases how customers have used their products to solve various problems[81], including things like how to displace moisture from your jet ski spark plugs, using it to remove crayon stains, or the time a bus driver in Asia used WD-40 to remove a python that was coiled around the undercarriage of his bus! If you have discovered a great use for their products, you can submit it and get featured on their website yourself. And this approach works; WD-40 has a fan club with 125,000 members. Does your product or company make people so happy that they form fan clubs in your honor?

Help customers track and celebrate their progress

Here's a joke I heard recently:

How do you know if someone does CrossFit?

Don't worry, they will tell you!

CrossFit is yet another hugely successful exercise phenomenon to come out of the US, but what sets it apart is how effective it is in turning gym goers into fans. CrossFitters are notorious for telling everyone around them about their latest personal records, how tough their latest workout was, and how much their muscles hurt at any given time. People, only somewhat jokingly, call it CultFit for the passionate devotion it creates in many people[VI].

One of the most successful CrossFit operators in the world is CrossFit Copenhagen, which opened in 2008 and as of mid-2017 has 21 locations across Denmark and over 15,000 members. Their two founders, Andreas Bang and Klaus Vesti, have a huge focus on helping people become stronger and healthier and have come up with some very simple ways to give their customers a feeling of results and celebrate their progress, including these:

- There's a bell in every exercise room that you ring when you set a new personal record—after which everyone in the class applauds you.
- They encourage their coaches to share and celebrate members' hard work and progress on social media.
- When you've attended a certain number of classes (10,

VI Yes, I do CrossFit too, but at least I waited until this far into the book before telling you about it.

50, 100 times, and so on), you get an email congratulating you on your hard work. The email includes a picture of a fist, and you're encouraged to fist bump your screen.

Happy leaders don't care only about their own progress or that of their company—they care deeply about the progress of their customers. If you can help your customers see the progress your products and services help them achieve, your offerings also look more valuable and they are more likely to stay customers. These stories of customer progress are also great to bring back to employees because it shows that their work is actually making a positive difference.

Help your customers help others

Ever seen a promotion like this?

For every shampoo bottle sold, we will donate 25 cents to rainforest preservation in South America!

Many companies do promotions where they promise to donate a certain amount to a worthy cause for every product sold or something similar. While it's nice that a company cares, I've honestly never felt particularly happy about any of these programs and they leave me feeling no better about the company, its products, or myself for being a customer.

London-based Innocent Drinks (who make tremendous smoothies and juices) came up with a much cooler idea that involves their customers directly in charity, called the "Innocent Big Knit." They invite people to knit little woolly hats that will fit on the caps of Innocent's small smoothie bottles and send them to the company. Innocent collects all the hats and puts them on smoothie bottles that are then sold in stores and donates 25p for every hat to a charity called Age UK, which helps the elderly[82]. The Big Knit website even features a section called "Meet the knitters" where they celebrate some of their top knitters, including two lovely retired teachers called Ali and Marion from Gosport who have so far contributed a whopping

2,500 little hats between them[83].

Since the program started in 2003, people have knitted an astonishing 6 million hats, raising over £1.9m for charity, which is amazing in itself, but beyond that it also gives Innocent's customers a chance to create results by making something that contributes directly to a worthy cause and relationships because many of them meet up and knit together.

Do what's right for the customer

What do you do when a customer calls asking for a product that is currently out of stock? Zappos is an online shoe and clothing retailer with 1,500 employees based in Las Vegas. Their Chief of Staff, Jamie Naughton, explained to me what they do:

> *If a customer is looking for something and we don't have it we will help them find it from a competitor site. So if you called looking for a size 10 Nike in a certain style and we didn't have it we will do a quick google search and look for someone who does have it and help direct you there to buy it.*
>
> *We know that in the short-term we are losing that customer's purchase, but in the long-term they*

remember the level of service we provided and then come back the next time they need something.

Yes, Zappos actually trains customer service employees to check competitors' websites to see if a product is available there and *actively send the customer to a competitor* because it's the best thing for the customer in that situation and maintains a better relationship with them.

A happy leader has to be able to put the company's own interests aside and do what's right for the customer. There is no way to build lasting, positive relationships with customers if you're just trying to wring as much money as possible out of them in any transaction. This means that happy leaders make sure that:

- You sell a customer only what they want and need—not as much you can make them buy.
- If your products and services are not right for the customer, send them somewhere else.
- If you make a mistake that harms the customer in some way, own the consequences.

This not only makes the customers happier, more loyal, and more likely to come back but also affects you and your employees, who can all feel proud to work for a company that does the right thing.

My all-time favorite example of this comes from the previously mentioned and rather unfortunately named Middelfart Savings Bank. Before the financial crisis, when all kinds of risky investments were booming, Middelfart had been very conservative and careful about where they advised their customers to put their money. However, they did recommend one particular bond called Scandinotes, which was marketed as a very safe and solid investment but ended up being completely worthless.

Many Danish banks had recommended the same investment to their customers, and 4,000 Danes ended up losing a total of nearly $150 million. The message from all the other banks to their customers was, essentially, "Too bad." They pointed to the terms of purchase which said that while the bank may have recommended the investment, each investor was personally responsible for any losses.

Middelfart Savings Bank weren't sure what to do, so they convened a meeting of the responsible people from each branch. They recommended that the right thing to do was to take responsibility for their bad advice and cover all of their customers' losses, which would cost the bank a whopping $4.5 million. The CEO and the board agreed, and that's what they ended up doing as the only bank in the country. The CEO at the time, Hans Erik Brønserud, said that it was simply a question of ethics to him:

> *When we haven't sufficiently advised our customers on the risks of these bonds, we haven't lived up to the bank's values.*

This is courageous, honest, and admirable behavior. That's how a leader shows that they're serious about their values: By living up to them even when the cost is high. Incidentally, the bank never went to the media and bragged about what they'd done. They did it quietly and with no fanfare and the story only came to light when one of their (understandably) happy customers shared what had happened with a journalist.

Have fun with your customers

> If you've ever been to an IKEA store on a Saturday, you know how busy they can get. Shopping carts everywhere, long lines at check out, hordes of children running around, and couples fighting over whether to get the VIMLE or the KLIPPAN couch.
>
> One IKEA store had a Saturday coming up that they knew was going to be one of the busiest shopping days of the year, and the head of the bedroom department told me that he wanted to make sure that this day would still be fun for both employees and customers. So, he came up with some cool ideas.
>
> All the employees in his team put on bathrobes over their uniforms, to make the whole thing more fun and informal. They also put up a sign announcing a pillow fight at noon

and ended up with 40 people (customers and employees) banging away on each other with pillows. The department leader himself spent part of the day hiding in one of the big PAX wardrobes and whenever a customer opened the door to check out the insides he stepped out with a big smile and said, "Yes, can I help you?"

Having fun is a great way to make customers happy and connect with them. Exactly how to do it depends on your team and what business you're in. If you run a funeral home, I would not recommend hiding in the coffins and jumping out at people. But the vast majority of workplaces offer at least some potential for having plain old fun with the customers, which when done right can brighten a lot of people's day.

We do this at our company. We have a monthly budget called The Woohoo Account for having fun with customers, partners and suppliers. We've invited them to things like a movie at a local cinema (incidentally, we showed "Horrible Bosses", which is hilarious), a backstage tour of the national aquarium, and a huge party featuring the world's happiest DJ.

Southwest Airlines are huge on fun. I've flown them myself and seen firsthand how open, friendly, and playful their staff are. Some do the pre-flight safety messages in a song or rap form, some play games with the passengers, and some hide in the overhead compartments to startle passengers. One ramp agent in Las Vegas, Jerico Nazareno, regularly breaks out his ukulele to play for the passengers waiting to board a plane[84]. In my opinion, flying on most airlines is, at best, a neutral experience; neither good nor bad. With Southwest, I actively look forward to flying.

Random acts of customer kindness

Berendsen is a huge multinational company that provides textile maintenance services to businesses. They supply towels, hospital uniforms, door mats, floor mops, and many other products to their customers, pick them up when they're dirty, launder them, and bring them back clean.

Kræn Nielsen, the Head of the Danish division, told me that traditionally, they'd been very focused on costs and logistics and kept very tight control of what their customer-facing employees could or could not do. In 2013, he decided to fundamentally change that approach and focus on doing random acts of kindness for Berendsen's customers.

At a two-day kickoff training, their 90 salespeople and customer service staff were introduced to the concept and the purpose behind it. The goal was to let the customers see a different side of Berendsen, going from a very rational to a more emotional approach.

He never told his employees what specifically to do, but here are some of the things they came up with.

One employee saw that a client (a famous cereal company) was celebrating a company anniversary, so he arranged the delivery of red carpets for their event. The customer called to ask who'd ordered it and how much it cost and was delighted to hear that "It's free. We just wanted to help you celebrate your milestone." A week later that client sent over a crate of their products for Berendsen's employees to enjoy, cementing a stronger relationship.

One customer called to say that they needed some more floor mops on short notice. Their next scheduled delivery was a few days away, and the distribution team didn't have the capacity to make an extra stop that day. One employee heard that, and she picked up the mops, got on her bike, and made a detour past the client on her way home from work. They were very surprised and very happy to get their mops delivered the same day by bicycle.

In a short time, the employees committed hundreds of random acts of customer kindness. One Berendsen employee brought some sunscreen for a customer who was going on vacation, one brought vegetables from his own garden, and one even managed to help a customer with an IT problem, which is not part of their usual laundry tasks.

Top management supported this new process in several ways:

- They gave each customer service employee a monthly "love budget" that they had to spend on customers. This was necessary because their employees had been trained to spend as little as possible otherwise.

- They put up a big transparent cylinder in the office. Every time an employee did a random act of customer kindness, they could throw a plastic ball in the cylinder, and once it was full, they took the whole team to an amusement park to celebrate.
- Each team created a Wall of Fame where they shared positive stories, praise, and emails from customers.
- Every month, the top management highlighted their favorite example of a random act of customer kindness and celebrated the employee responsible.
- The best stories were collected and published in a booklet.

> Not only did all of this make the customers happier, but it also turned out to have an equally positive effect on the employees, who really enjoyed their new freedom to spread happiness. It even spread to the point where employees did random acts of kindness for each other.
>
> I asked Kræn what his most important personal learning was and he said "The essence is, that you don't have to do something huge to make a difference. It's the personal and emotional connection to the client that makes a difference."

I also worked with Telenor, a Scandinavian telecommunications company, on a campaign that was rolled out to all their stores in Denmark just before Christmas in 2015. Every store employee received ten postcards that they had to send out to customers with a handwritten message during December, which led to many positive customer reactions. One elderly lady from Latin America came into a Telenor store looking for help with her cell phone plan. It turned out that one of the young men working there spoke Spanish, so he sent her a nice postcard in Spanish, which she really enjoyed.

Doing these nice, small, surprising things for customers can create a lot of happiness. One story from Zappos shows just how much. A customer was supposed to return some shoes but had failed to do so because her mother had died. Then this happened:

When I came home this last time, I had an email from Zappos asking about the shoes, since they hadn't received them. I was just back and not ready to deal with that, so I replied that my mom had died but that I'd send the shoes as soon as I could. They emailed back that they had arranged with UPS to pick up the shoes, so I wouldn't have to take the time to do it myself. I was so touched. That's going against corporate policy.

Yesterday, when I came home from town, a florist delivery man was just leaving. It was a beautiful arrangement in a basket with white lilies and roses and carnations. Big and lush and fragrant. I opened the card, and it was from Zappos. I burst into tears. I'm a sucker for kindness, and if that isn't one of the nicest things I've ever had happen to me, I don't know what is.

Let your employees be themselves

McDonald's restaurants are famous for having rules for everything, including how to take an order, how to pack the order, how to wash your hands before your shift, and much more. This standardization has helped make them effective and profitable.

But McDonald's Denmark realized that they could make their customers happier if they gave their employees a little more freedom to be themselves. They launched a new service concept called "Vital Ingredients" that included elements like "Enjoy What You Do" and "Be You." Mette Hybschmann, their head of HR, told me how this created room for their employees to do things like organize flash mobs in the restaurants or compete on celebrity sightings. The whole thing was centered around "Serving happy moments" to customers.

Some companies try to create good customer service by creating elaborate scripts and rules for their employees. I think that's a trap, because taking away employees' freedom to be themselves makes them unhappy, inevitably reducing the quality of customer service. Zappos has no phone scripts for their customer services employees to read from. Tony Hsieh, their CEO, explained it like this[85]:

> *We don't have scripts, because we want our reps to let their true personalities shine during every phone call, so that they can develop a personal emotional connection with each customer.*

Instead of mandating every single aspect of customer interactions, train your employees incredibly well on what kind of experience you want to give your customers, and then give them the freedom to do it their own way. Yes, occasionally they will get it wrong, and a customer may complain, but on the whole, they will give much better, happier, and more authentic customer service.

Measure your employees on customer happiness

I stayed at a hotel in Cape Town a while back for a speaking trip, and after my stay, they sent me the usual customer satisfaction survey, which had 43 questions like "How satisfied were you with the check-in experience?", "How satisfied were you with the location of the hotel?", and even (I'm not kidding) "How satisfied were you with the light in your room?" Needless to say, this survey was too long, and I gave up long before I'd completed it, but more than that, it also measured the wrong thing, focusing squarely on customer satisfaction, not customer happiness.

A t Zappos, they have a much simpler way to measure customer happiness. Jamie Naughton, their Chief of Staff, told me that after every call, email, or chat you get a chance to answer this question:

> *"Do you feel that the Zappos family member you interacted with genuinely cares about you and your reason for contacting us?" [Yes or No]*

There are three reasons why this one question is much more

useful:

1. It's a simple, clear question.
2. It is emotional, asking "do you feel that...," and therefore much better at gauging customer happiness.
3. It is relational, asking if the employee cared about the customer and their situation.

Once that question is answered, the customer is directed to a web page that has three additional questions where the customer rates aspects of Zappos' service from 1 to 5:

- The eagerness of the Zappos team member to help
- The quality of solutions provided by the Zappos team member
- The Zappos team member's knowledge of products and services we offer
- Additional Feedback (Optional)

Zappos customer service employees are consistently measured and trained on these factors.

Some leaders get this completely wrong. They tell employees to give great service and make customers happy, but then they measure employees on how many customers they handle or on their sales numbers.

If you tell your employees that you want them to make the customers happy, but then measure them on completely different metrics, you're not only setting them up to fail; you're also creating a lot of employee unhappiness because you say one thing but do another. Sadly, many companies measure employees on volume (how many customers they handle) or cost (how cheaply they do it).

Handling as many customer requests as possible as cheaply as possible is clearly not compatible with giving each customer full attention and great service. The problem with measuring service volume is that it encourages the wrong behavior. An employee who is measured on call volume is incentivized to keep calls as short as possible and do everything they can to avoid handling more complicated or difficult cases. And when a leader says one thing but measures another, it's the one that is measured that people take seriously. That's why it makes a lot more sense to measure customer happiness instead.

Dipali Sikand is the founder of a company in India called Les Concierges. Her 700 employees deliver concierge services to the employees of their corporate clients—helping them with everything from restaurant reservations to laundry services. Her employees go above and beyond for the clients many times every day, and she told me that they found an incredibly simple way to keep track of and celebrate the best examples of great customer service: They created a WhatsApp group called "Moments of WOW." All employees and managers are members of this group, and every time an employee does something cool for a client or receives positive feedback from a happy customer; they can share it to this group. All the other members of the group see it, and thus best practices and positive moments quickly spread inside the company.

Connect with customers

I love Disney World and have been to the parks in Orlando and Paris several times. The last time I was at Disney World in Orlando, we drove up to one of the parking lots in our rental car, and after I paid for parking, the Disney employee in the booth looked at my wife and said, "Wow, you have a lovely smile, Ma'am." First of all, it's true—she absolutely does have a lovely smile. But secondly, what a great thing to notice and say! And this kind of interaction is no coincidence. Disney World takes great pains to teach their employees the value of connecting with the guests[VII].

Every interaction you or your employees have with a customer is a chance to connect with that person and make them a little happier by doing simple things like giving them a compliment, finding a shared interest, or cracking a joke. Just seeing the customer, and particularly seeing something positive in them, can make a difference and brighten a person's day in a world where more and more people feel isolated and lonely.

Even if a customer is calling in to complain, you can connect with them. Innocent Drinks print a customer service number on

VIIYou're not a customer at Disney World, you're a guest.

every one of their bottles or cartons, and if you, as a drinker (what they call their customers), have any complaints or questions, you can call that number, and it will ring every phone in their London HQ. Yes, instead of outsourcing complaints to a customer service team, they train all their employees to answer those calls and get the details needed to give that customer a refund or whatever may be needed. And they also teach their people to send a fun, handwritten letter to the drinker afterward.

You can train your employees to do this, but you, as a leader, can also do it yourself every chance you get. Craig Newmark, founder of the incredibly successful classified advertisements website Craigslist, says his most important job as a leader is in direct customer support[86]:

> *In starting Craigslist, way back in '95, I assumed a direct customer support mission.*
>
> *That put me in direct contact with thousands of people, mostly Americans, who needed basics, like help putting food on the table, getting that table, getting a roof to put the table under.*
>
> *Direct customer service like that means getting in touch and staying in touch with regular people in a way that I, as an old-school nerd, never did.*
>
> *Overall, I've delegated myself into uselessness; I still do just enough customer service to stay in touch with the needs of regular people.*

In his time as the CEO of JetBlue, David Neeleman saw every flight he took as an opportunity to connect with the passengers. At the beginning of the flight, he would introduce himself as the CEO of the company and ask the passengers to share any thoughts, concerns, or feedback with him. He would then come through the cabin serving snacks and even had his own apron with the title "Snack Boy" embroidered on it. Neeleman is now introducing the same culture at Azul, the airline he founded in Brazil.

Help customers in difficult situations

DaVita is an American company that has about 2,000 clinics all over America where 160,000 patients come to get dialysis treatments. If you know someone with failing kidneys, you know that getting dialysis is tough physically and mentally. However, it's what keeps you alive. If you don't get dialysis for just a few days, it becomes life-threatening.

This became critical after Hurricane Katrina hit New Orleans because many patients couldn't get to the DaVita clinics for their dialysis. DaVita employee Brian Applewhite describes one attempt to locate a patient[87]:

> The first thing we did after the storm was start looking for our patients, and I literally had to cut through trees to find them.
>
> There was one lady that we called Mrs. B. She lived in a low-income area, and I was walking through the streets screaming her name, but no one was responding. I remembered that she once told me that people called her "Big Mama," so I tried screaming that.
>
> They pointed me to the house with the big tree on it! Big Mama hadn't dialyzed in three days, and when I walked in, she said she thought she'd seen a ghost.

Brian got Mrs. B to dialysis in time, and she made it. Two things stand out to me about this story. First, that an employee will go to such lengths for a customer. Going out into post-hurricane New Orleans must have been daunting, to say the least. But also, the reason he found Mrs. B at all was that he knew her well enough personally to know that she was also called Big Mama. He had a relationship with her that was more than just transactional—it was personal.

You, as a leader, can sometimes directly help customers in tough situations, but more than that, you can set your employees free to do it when they see a chance to help. When employees go above and beyond to do something like this, happy leaders treat them like the heroes they are for helping customers when they need it most.

My favorite example of this comes from Southwest Airlines,

in a story first shared by consumer advocate Christopher Elliott[88]. A grandfather was traveling to Denver for the most tragic reason imaginable: His three-year-old grandson had been murdered and was being taken off life support at 9 pm, and his organs were being donated to 25 people, saving many lives.

He got to LAX two hours early, but the lines for security were endless. He tried explaining his situation, but no one would listen. Finally, he made it through security and ran to the gate on stocking feet, shoes in hand, even though he knew that it was too late and that the plane should have left by now.

When he got to the gate, he found the pilot of his plane waiting for him with the words, "Are you Mark? We held the plane for you, and we're so sorry about the loss of your grandson." They knew about his situation because his wife had booked the ticket and explained the situation to the ticketing agent.

As he walked down the Jetway with the pilot, he said, "I can't thank you enough for this." The pilot responded with, "They can't go anywhere without me, and I wasn't going anywhere without you. Now, relax. We'll get you there. And again, I'm so sorry."

Holding back a plane is expensive and can cause further delays. So, how did the company react when they learned what the pilot had done? Southwest spokeswoman Marilee McInnis said[89]:

> *I think we would all agree that the pilot absolutely made the right decision. I don't think you could ask for a better example of great service for our customers.*
>
> *As you're reading the story, you absolutely get tears in your eyes and just an overwhelming sense of pride that our pilot took such an action. It really makes you proud to work for Southwest.*

This kind of behavior is directly related to happiness at work. First of all, happy employees are much more likely to do such acts. If you love your job and are having a great day, you are much more likely to notice customers in need of aid and act to help them. But the effect also goes the other way: Being able to help others makes us happier (as we've seen again and again), and working for a company that actively helps those in need gives employees a sense of pride and meaning in their work.

The customer is not always right

This story comes from the amazing book "Nuts!" by Jackie and Kevin Freiberg:

> One woman who frequently flew on Southwest was constantly disappointed with every aspect of the company's operation. In fact, she became known as the "Pen Pal" because after every flight she wrote in with a complaint.
>
> She didn't like the fact that the company didn't assign seats; she didn't like the absence of a first-class section; she didn't like not having a meal in flight; she didn't like Southwest's boarding procedure; she didn't like the flight attendants' sporty uniforms and the casual atmosphere.
>
> Her last letter, reciting a litany of complaints, momentarily stumped Southwest's customer relations people. They bumped it up to Herb's [Kelleher, CEO of Southwest at the time] desk, with a note: 'This one's yours.'
>
> In sixty seconds, Kelleher wrote back and said, 'Dear Mrs. Crabapple, We will miss you. Love, Herb.'"

The phrase "The customer is always right" was originally coined in 1909 by Harry Gordon Selfridge, the founder of Selfridges department store in London, and is typically used by businesses to convince customers that they will get good service at this company and convince employees to give customers good service.

However, I think leaders should abandon this phrase once and for all—ironically because it leads to worse customer service. Here are the top five reasons why "The Customer Is Always Right" is wrong.

1: It Makes Employees Unhappy

Gordon Bethune is a brash Texan (as is Herb Kelleher, coincidentally) who is best known for turning Continental Airlines around "From Worst to First," a story told in his book of the same title from 1998. He wanted to make sure that both customers and employees liked the way Continental treated them, so he made it very clear that the maxim "The customer is always right" didn't hold sway at Continental. In conflicts between the employees and unruly customers, he would consistently side with his people. Here's how he put it:

> *When we run into customers that we can't reel back in, our loyalty is with our employees. They have to put up with this stuff every day. Just because you buy a ticket does not give you the right to abuse our employees...*
>
> *We run more than 3 million people through our books every month. One or two of those people are going to be unreasonable, demanding jerks. When it's a choice between supporting your employees, who work with you every day and make your product what it is, or some irate jerk who demands a free ticket to Paris because you ran out of peanuts, whose side are you going to be on?*
>
> *You can't treat your employees like serfs. You have to value them... If they think that you won't support them when a customer is out of line, even the smallest problem can cause resentment.*

So, Bethune trusted his people over unreasonable customers. What I like about this attitude is that it balances employees and customers. The "always right" maxim squarely favors the customer, which is a bad idea, because, as Bethune says, it causes resentment among employees.

When the leader sides with customers over employees who were just doing their jobs and enforcing the rules, employees see it as a clear betrayal that is extremely demotivating. It creates strong feelings of unfairness and injustice, which we saw on page 34 affects the brain the same way physical pain does.

Of course, there are plenty of examples of bad employees giving lousy customer service but trying to solve this by declaring the customer "always right" is counter-productive.

2: It Gives Abrasive Customers an Unfair Advantage

Using the slogan "The customer is always right," abusive customers can demand just about anything—they're right by definition, aren't they? This makes the employees' jobs that much harder when trying to rein them in. Also, it means that abusive customers get better treatment and conditions than nice customers. That always seemed wrong to me, and it makes much more sense to be nice to the nice customers to keep them coming back.

3: Some Customers Are Bad for Business

Many leaders think that "The more customers we have, the better." But some customers are quite simply bad for business. Danish IT service provider ServiceGruppen proudly tells this story:

> *One of our service technicians arrived at a customer's site for a maintenance task, and to his great shock was treated very rudely by the customer.*
>
> *When he'd finished the task and returned to the office, he told the management about his experience. They promptly cancelled the customer's contract.*

Just like Kelleher dismissed the irate lady who kept complaining (but somehow also kept flying Southwest), ServiceGruppen fired a bad customer. Note that it was not even a matter of a financial calculation—not a question of whether the company would make or lose money on that customer in the long run. It was a simple matter of respect and dignity and of treating their employees right.

4: It Results in Worse Customer Service

Rosenbluth International took it even further. As I mentioned on page 94, they actually put their employees first and customers second. Their CEO, Hal Rosenbluth, argued that when you put the employees first, they put the customers first.

Put employees first, and they will be happy at work. Employees who are happy at work give better customer service because they care more about other people, will go the extra mile for customers, have more energy, and are more fun to talk to and interact with.

On the other hand, when the company and management consistently side with customers instead of with employees, it sends a clear message that employees are not valued, should not expect to be treated fairly, have no right to respectful treatment, and must put up with everything from customers. When this attitude prevails, employees stop caring about service. At that point, genuinely good service is almost impossible—the best customers can hope for is fake good service. You know the kind I mean: courteous on the surface only.

5: Some Customers Are Just Plain Wrong

Herb Kelleher agrees, as this passage from "Nuts!" shows:

> *Herb Kelleher [...] makes it clear that his employees come first—even if it means dismissing customers. But aren't customers always right? "No, they are not," Kelleher snaps. "And I think that's one of the biggest betrayals of employees a boss can possibly commit. The customer is sometimes wrong. We don't carry those sorts of customers. We write to them and say, 'Fly somebody else. Don't abuse our people.'"*

The fact is that some customers are just plain wrong; businesses are better off without them. Managers siding with unreasonable customers over employees is a very bad idea that makes employees unhappy and results in worse customer service.

In the quest for happier customers, it is tempting to put the customer first. Don't. Leaders should put their employees first, so that they can put the customer first.

This chapter in tweets

- Go beyond customer satisfaction—make your customers'

lives happier, safer, healthier, richer, more fun, or better in some other way.

- Forget how awesome your product is. Focus on how awesome your customer is when they use your product.
- Do what's best for the customer—not what's best for your short-term profits.
- Don't be afraid to have fun with your customers. The happy ones will enjoy it, and it might even scare off the unpleasant customers.
- Do random acts of kindness for your customers—it creates a lot of happiness.
- Happy employees naturally give great service and make the customers happier.
- Some companies have elaborate rules for customer service. That's a trap. Train your employees well, then set them free to be themselves.
- Measure and evaluate your service employees on customer happiness before anything else.
- Connect with customers. Every interaction is a chance to connect with that person and make them a little happier.
- "The Customers is Always Right" is wrong. Support your employees against unreasonable demands from rude customers.

Make the world happy

The corporate world means nothing unless it improves the lives of people and the conditions in poor countries.

–Dr. Haldor Topsøe

The final group we're going to look at is the world outside the organization. The focus can be on the local community, on a disadvantaged group, on preserving the environment, or it can be the wider world.

I also include the investors in this category. Whether they are shareholders, company founders, angel investors, or similar, keeping them happy is clearly important—but not all-important. They are one group out of the many that leaders should aim to keep happy. Here's how to spread happiness to the wider world outside the organization.

Have a vision for happiness

Vega IT Sourcing based in Novi Sad in Serbia has one of the most beautiful corporate visions I've seen painted in big letters on one wall in their building:

It is our dream to create a happy and successful business, allowing us to use its success and power to make the world a better place.

And these are not just pretty words; this is something they take very seriously. Sasa Popovic, their CEO and co-founder, told me about the many things they do to make that happen:

- They give scholarships for poor children to go to school.
- They promote entrepreneurship in the local community. They believe that a business is only as strong as the community it supports. This has already resulted in the creation of several new companies in Novi Sad.
- Their "Giving back to the community program" allows anyone from Vega IT to start an internal campaign for a cause. Whatever amount the employees collect, the company doubles.
- Their "Code for a Cause" campaign lets their developers and designers build apps or systems to improve the lives of people in the local community. Vega IT organizes the campaign and covers all costs, and the finished systems are open-sourced and given to non-profit organizations or local public institutions.
- They arrange many open charity events, e.g. a foosball tournament for all IT companies in town to raise money for an MRI machine for a children's hospital.

The result is that Vega IT's 135 employees are proud and happy to work there. They do great work for the clients and the company has won a number of awards including top five most desirable employers in Serbia and the 2016 Golden Gazelle Serbia Award for being "Best among the most dynamically growing companies in Serbia."

It's easy to get the corporate vision wrong. I delivered a speech at the London Business School some years back and their vision, proudly engraved on a plaque in the lobby, was: "We want to be the leading business school in the world." Can you spot the mistake? That's not a vision, that's a goal. A good vision is bigger than the organization and clearly makes the world better somehow.

The pharmaceutical company Xellia, one of our clients, also display their vision in the lobby, but they got it right:

> *"Our purpose is to save lives by leading the fight against infection."*

As you may know, one of the biggest current medical crises is the increasing risk of infection by multi-resistant bacteria that are immune to traditional antibiotics. Xellia produces an antibiotic that is still effective against multi-resistant bacteria and therefore their research and products directly save lives all over the world.

Xellia have the advantage that their products improve peoples' health and save lives. But what if your company doesn't in itself directly make the world better? You can still have a positive vision. Here are some great examples.

- The Danish mobile phone company CallMe has dedicated themselves to improving the way people communicate. They created a wildly successful campaign called "Talk Nicely," which is all about reducing bullying and making people interact in a friendlier, calmer, and happier way. Their CEO at the time, Hanne Lindblad, stated that in an industry where everyone else competes mainly on price, they wanted to stand for something meaningful.
- Southwest Airlines' mission is to "Connect people to what's important in their lives through friendly, reliable, and low-cost air travel."
- Patagonia's mission is all about improving the environment: "Build the best product, cause no unnecessary harm, use business to inspire and implement solutions to the environmental crisis."

Of course, it's not enough to have a beautiful vision—the company must live up to it. If it doesn't actually live by it, it's better not to have the vision in the first place.

Ultimately, a good company vision is all about happiness because the end goal will improve the lives of people outside the organization. It's easy to see, in each of the examples above, how they are directly making people happier. This does not mean that the company ignores profits—it just means that the company must find a path to profits that supports the vision. A company that can't figure out how to run their business in a way that makes the world better and happier shouldn't be in business at all.

Give more than just money

> In many Danish companies, there is a tradition of giving employees a nice Christmas present. As long as the price of the gift is below DKK 800 (about $120), employees receive it tax-free so most companies will go to that limit. Sadly, very few Danish employees are particularly happy about these presents—it's become yet another expected perk or entitlement. In fact, some employees even complain when the present is something they don't want or already own.
>
> The Danish startup Sprout makes these wonderful pencils you can plant when you're done with them and grow tomatoes, herbs, flowers, or something similar. Two of their employees took leadership one year by asking "What if we donate our Christmas present budget to a local orphanage?"
>
> The colleagues at Sprout agreed, and the CEO even offered to double the amount—but here's the really cool part: Instead of just donating the money, the employees involved themselves directly. They got every child at the orphanage to write a wish list, went to a toy store, and bought every single child something from that list, gift wrapped them, and delivered them in person. That was a lot more meaningful and made them much happier than just writing a check with a donation.

Many companies do good in the world by donating to charities. My company has committed to donating 10% of our profits every year, which we usually send to Doctors Without Borders because we admire their work so much.

Next Jump also encourages charitable giving. For instance, after hurricane Sandy, many low-wage New Yorkers couldn't work and therefore lost crucial income. Next Jumpers gave 10% of their paychecks to these "Forgotten Ones" and started handing out envelopes of cash with a note explaining where this money came from.

But a company can also contribute something much more valuable: your and your employees' time, skill, and passion. Charlie Kim, the CEO of Next Jump, told me how his company adopted a school in 2015, but rather than just donating money to the school, Next Jump's people have involved themselves directly in training both the teachers and the kids.

Here's an idea: Make your next team-building event more meaningful by going out and helping someone else. Instead of an event where the team cooks a gourmet meal for itself, make sandwiches to distribute to the homeless in your city. Instead of building a raft and sailing it across a lake (after which the raft is immediately disassembled), renovate a classroom at a local school.

Sustainability and beyond

Many companies are trying to be more environmentally sustainable, for instance by recycling paper, by urging employees to turn off the lights, or by reducing consumption in production. But some leaders are taking it even further. Instead of defining sustainability as "not doing harm to the environment", they adopt a policy of "net-positive environmental impact," so that their company as a whole leaves the environment better than if the company did not exist.

Black Friday, the biggest US shopping day, is the Friday after Thanksgiving where many retailers offer special deals and promotions. So, why did Patagonia run a big ad on Black Friday in 2015 with a picture of one of their jackets and a big headline that said, "Don't buy this jacket?" Here's how they explained it in the ad:[90]

> *It's time for us as a company to address the issue of consumerism and do it head-on.*
>
> *The most challenging and important element of the Common Threads Initiative is this: to lighten our environmental footprint, everyone needs to consume less. Businesses need to make fewer things but of higher quality. Customers need to think twice before they buy.*

The ad urged people to reduce their consumption in four ways:

- REDUCE: WE make useful gear that lasts a long time—YOU don't buy what you don't need.
- REPAIR: WE help you repair your Patagonia gear—YOU pledge to fix what's broken.
- REUSE: WE help find a home for Patagonia gear you no longer need—YOU sell or pass it on (eBay is a great place to start).
- RECYCLE: WE will take back your Patagonia gear that is worn out—YOU pledge to keep your stuff out of the landfill and incinerator.

As we saw previously, Patagonia's mission is to "Build the best product, cause no unnecessary harm, use business to inspire and implement solutions to the environmental crisis." This all comes from their founder Yvon Chouinard, who has a burning passion for the environment that affects every aspect of the business. Here are just some of the ways they act on it:

- Since 1985, Patagonia has donated 1% of its sales to environmental organizations and started a charity called "1% For the Planet", which encourages businesses and individuals to do the same.
- Employees can take time off for environmental activism.
- When they couldn't find organic cotton for their products, they invested directly in several cotton farms to help them switch from regular farming to organic.
- In 2016, they donated their entire Black Friday sales, about $10 million, to environmental organizations.

Patagonia has also joined the B Corp movement[91], an association of organizations that have committed to the following Declaration of Interdependence:

> *We envision a global economy that uses business as a force for good.*
>
> *This economy is comprised of a new type of business—the B corporation—which is purpose-driven and creates benefits for all stakeholders, not just shareholders.*

As B Corporations and leaders of this emerging economy, we believe:

- *That we must be the change we seek in the world.*
- *That all business must be conducted as if people and place mattered.*
- *That, through their products, practices, and profits, businesses should aspire to do no harm and benefit all.*
- *To do so requires that we act with the understanding that we are each dependent upon another and thus responsible for each other and future generations.*

More than 2,100 companies from 50 countries and over 130 industries are certified B Corps and therefore directly committed to creating a happier planet through business.

Make suppliers, vendors, and partners happy

Ben and Jerry's have this beautiful mission statement that directly includes treating their suppliers well:

Create linked prosperity for everyone that's connected to our business: suppliers, employees, farmers, franchisees, customers, and neighbors alike.

They recognize that they can make a positive difference for their suppliers of vanilla, milk, cocoa, and so on around the world and are happy to pay a premium for the products. Here's an example from their website[92]:

The Huatusco Coffee Cooperative in Mexico supplies us with much of our Fairtrade coffee—since 2010, we have sourced more than 300,000 pounds of coffee from them for our flavors. Our social premiums are helping the cooperative's 1,465 farmers, along with their families and communities, in many ways. It has contributed to the construction of a medical center, a library, and schools; the development of scholarships and education projects; and the production of 400 tons of compost.

Why not be nice to your vendors and suppliers? Instead of seeing it as an adversarial relationship where the goal is to squeeze them for everything you can, treat them as a valuable and integral part of the ecosystem your organization exists in.

Zappos sees their vendors and suppliers as an important part of their world and do everything they can to make them happy, including throwing them a huge annual vendor party in Las Vegas. They said this about their 2016 vendor party[93]:

Vendors are our friends behind the brands you see on Zappos.com. Every exciting item you lay your eyes on has someone diligently working with us to ensure you get the best quality, the best selection and the best price. We couldn't do what we do without them, and each year we want to make sure they feel the love. With many of them in town at once, what better way to show our gratitude than one enormous, crazy, over-the-top Zappos bash?

"The personal side of just hanging out with our vendor partners and having fun together builds stronger relationships," says Mike Normart, one of Zappos' merchandising gurus. "So many vendors change jobs frequently, and you never know where they will end up. Time and time again we have added brands because of the great relationships we have built over the years with our vendors."

Former no title executive Fred Mossler, who recently left the company but joined Zappos in 1999, knows first-hand business is the result of bonding. "Too many other retailers treat the vendor relationship as adversarial or transactional," said Mossler. "We are the only retailer to throw a party for our vendors."

At the party, they also gave out the "Rep of the Year" award. Four vendors were nominated for the prize each quarter, and all nominees were celebrated at the party by being given their own private cabana, and the final winner walked away with the honor and an amazing vacation.

Make unions happy

Another important constituency for leaders to focus on is trade unions and union reps. Leaders should build positive relationships with the unions that represent employees. Ultimately, everyone has an interest in the company being successful, and if you can find common ground around that, you can spend more time collaborating and less time fighting.

Make investors happy

> *Numbers and money follow; they do not lead.*
>
> *–Dan Gilbert, CEO of Quicken Loans*

Yes, investors matter, and they're one constituency that a happy leader must be aware of. If the investors are not happy, it may be hard for the company to attract the capital it needs to grow and innovate.

Fortunately, as we've seen again and again throughout this book, happiness is good for business, and happy companies make more money. You'd think that if a company treats its employees well (a lot better than their competitors) and gets great business results because of it, that this company and its executives would be celebrated and praised for it. You'd be wrong. The New York Times ran a great article about Costco, the huge American chain of warehouses, who spend much more on their employees than their main competitors[94]:

> *Costco's average pay, for example, is $17 an hour, 42 percent higher than its fiercest rival, Sam's Club. And Costco's health plan makes those at many other retailers look Scroogish.*

According to Costco's CEO Jim Sinegal, this makes good business sense:

> *Good wages and benefits are why Costco has*

extremely low rates of turnover and theft by employees, he said. And Costco's customers, who are more affluent than other warehouse store shoppers, stay loyal because they like that low prices do not come at the workers' expense. "This is not altruistic," he said. "This is good business."

The results are pretty impressive—Costco has over 700 warehouses, 126,000 employees, and 2016 revenue of $118.7 billion. So, how do stock analysts react to this? They tell Costco to stop treating employees well:

Emme Kozloff, an analyst at Sanford C. Bernstein & Company, faulted Mr. Sinegal as being too generous to employees. "He has been too benevolent," she said. "He's right that a happy employee is a productive long-term employee, but he could force employees to pick up a little more of the burden."

This makes zero sense, but it perfectly illustrates that traditional business thinking still regards employees as resources, that, like any other corporate commodity, must be bought as cheaply as possible. Executives who believe in treating employees well are faced with pressure from analysts and the stock market to stop doing so and start being more like anyone else—regardless of the results their strategy has been getting them so far.

This makes it important to educate current and potential investors on the business value of happiness. They may simply not be aware of the clear link between happy employees and better financial results. But it may also be important to scare off investors who don't share the company's vision.

When Google had their IPO, the prospectus written for potential investors was very clear on one thing: Google's success comes in large part from treating employees well, and they're only going to focus more on that. Founders Sergey Brinn and Larry Page made it very clear that they would continue to run the company their way and promised to go on treating their employees extremely well and making long-term decisions rather than living from quarter to quarter. If investors didn't care for that, they were kindly requested to take their money elsewhere:

> *Our employees, who have named themselves Googlers, are everything. Google is organized around the ability to attract and leverage the talent of exceptional technologists and business people. We have been lucky to recruit many creative, principled, and hard-working stars. We hope to recruit many more in the future. We will reward and treat them well.*
>
> *We provide many unusual benefits for our employees, including meals free of charge, doctors, and washing machines. We are careful to consider the long-term advantages to the company of these benefits. Expect us to add benefits rather than pare them down over time. We believe it is easy to be penny wise and pound foolish with respect to benefits that can save employees considerable time and improve their health and productivity.*

"But wait a minute," you might argue. "The shareholders own the company, right? Doesn't that mean they come first?" It's a common belief, but the answer is a clear "No!" Legally, owning stock in a company entitles you to a share of dividends —that's all:

> *Shareholders do not have the right to manage the company in which they hold an interest, and even their right to appoint the people who do is largely theoretical. They are entitled only to such part of the income as the directors declare as dividends, and have no right to the proceeds of the sale of corporate assets — except in the event of the liquidation of the entire company, in which case they will get what is left; not much, as a rule*[95].

Southwest Airlines have also clearly demonstrated that their first priorities are their employees and encourage them to do amazing things that may not directly improve the bottom line, or may even cost money. At the 2008 Southwest Airlines

Shareholders' Meeting, CEO Gary Kelly ended his presentation with this story[96]:

> On February the 27th, we had flight number 1218 preparing for departure from Dallas to Las Vegas via Austin, and as the customers were taking their seats, our Dallas flight attendant Robin Hopkins was approached by a customer who I'll refer to as Janice.
>
> Janice was asking for help with her cell phone, and she didn't know how to turn it off. Robin assisted Janice but asked if she was okay because Robin could tell that she had been crying. Janice answered that she was on her way to Las Vegas to identify her only son at the medical examiner's office.
>
> Upon hearing this, Robin informed the two other flight attendants Melissa Smith and Lisa Christian as to what was going on and our flight attendants comforted Janice.
>
> Melissa and Lisa handled the entire flight from Austin to Las Vegas while Robin sat with Janice, and she learned about her son, and she was there to provide comfort. They talked for the rest of the flight.
>
> When they landed in Las Vegas, Candace Robinson and Brandy Fuller who are Las Vegas in-flight supervisors met Janice at the gate, and they took over. Brandy handled all of her immediate needs while Candace went on to get her own car to drive Janice. Candace was also able to secure a hotel room next to the funeral home.
>
> There was no one there for Janice except for Southwest Airlines people, and this is just one powerful example of our people in action, and it happens hundreds of times every single day, most of which we never hear about. But they don't do it for the recognition, they don't do it for the money. They do it because they care, and at Southwest Airlines we are blessed to find and to hire and to keep people who care.
>
> I don't know if you can teach people how to care, but you can encourage it, you can support it, and when you know about it, you can certainly recognize it.

Telling this kind of story at the shareholders' meeting sends a clear signal to Southwest's investors: Our company culture matters more than anything else, we celebrate employees who do this kind of thing, and you can be proud to invest in a company that makes a positive difference in the world.

Maybe—just maybe—making the investors happy involves more than just making them as much money as possible. We can definitely strive to do that, but we can also make them happier by leading our organizations in a way that has a positive impact in the world and then showing the investors that their investment *matters* and makes the world a better place.

This chapter in tweets

- A good company vision is all about happiness because the end goal will improve the lives of people outside the organization.
- Shareholders are not all-important. Make them happy by delivering sustainable profits in a way that improves the world.
- A company that can't figure out how to run their business in a way that makes the world better and happier shouldn't be in business at all.
- Good leaders go beyond sustainability (do no harm) and lead in a way that makes the world better.
- Don't treat vendors and supplies as adversaries and squeeze them for everything you can. Treat them as well as you treat your customers.
- The customer is not always right. Happy leaders stand up for their people
- Give money to charity but also give something much more valuable: your people's time, skill, and passion.
- If shareholders don't agree with your company's positive vision, find better shareholders.

Leading with happiness in tough times

"If you don't stick to your values when they're being tested, they're not values: they're hobbies."

- Jon Stewart on the first episode of The Daily Show after 9/11

How Xilinx got through its biggest crisis

When I first met Wim Roelandts back in 2008, the world economy was in a terrible state, but he wasn't really worried because, as he told me, that was his 8th recession so far, and it wasn't even the worst one.

Wim's worst crisis as a leader came in 2000 when his company Xilinx, a computer chip manufacturer based in California, got hit hard and fast by the dot-com implosion. In the December 2000 quarter, their revenue was $450 million, and nine months later, their revenue for the September 2001 quarter had plummeted to only $225 million.

Something had to be done—and fast. But what? Roelandts, an affable Belgian who is usually seen with a smile on his face, was the CEO back then (he's since retired) and was clearly facing some tough choices. All of Xilinx's competitors wasted little time in laying off large percentages of their staff to cut costs, but Wim felt that there had to be a better way. He came up with a plan for his organization and the 2,800 people in it and called it "Share the pain". The plan had three major components.

1: Cut salaries, not jobs

Wim felt strongly that if they laid off people now, they'd just need to rehire them 5 or 6 quarters later when business improved. Couldn't there be a way that kept people on even during the crisis?

So, they instituted a pay cut that was progressive and voluntary. Progressive meant that your pay cut depended on your salary—the higher your salary, the higher your pay cut. These were some typical pay cuts:

Job	Pay cut
Production-level employees	0%
Junior-level engineers	6%
Senior engineers and middle managers	9%
Directors	12%
Vice Presidents	15%
CEOs (Wim Roelandts himself)	20%

So, while production employees were not affected at all, Wim himself took the largest pay cut—20% of his salary. They could have given everyone a 10% pay cut, but chose this way because it shares the pain—not the pay cut. When you're a production-level employee with an annual salary of $30,000–40,000 trying to live in the Silicon Valley area, a 5% or 10% pay cut could really impact your financial situation. When you're a VP, 15% is entirely survivable.

The pay cut was voluntary. This wasn't part of the original plan but it turned out that Xilinx's European employees would have to agree to take the pay cut voluntarily due to labor laws, so Wim decided to make it voluntary for everyone.

Amazingly, every one of the 2,800 employees chose to take the pay cut—except one. And no, that one person was not singled out for reprisals of any kind. Voluntary means voluntary. Reflecting on that period, Wim was especially proud that his people were willing to take pay cuts in order to save their co-workers' jobs.

Later in the process, when the pay cuts turned out not to be enough to keep the company profitable, they introduced more measures, like closing the company for one day every other week and the option of taking a paid leave of absence to take part in an educational and training activities. Though Wim was very careful never to promise that there would be no layoffs, this plan meant that Xilinx got through the crisis without laying so much as one single employee.

2: Communicate openly

Wim knew that honest communication was essential. His motto was to keep communicating and force his management team to communicate. In practice, he organized meetings with his entire management staff and the managers under them as well. He knew that when employees had questions, they wouldn't come to him or the other executives, they would go to the managers closest to them, so it was important that they knew what was happening and remained optimistic.

This is not easy, as Wim readily admits:

> *"I didn't know any more than anybody else what was coming, and so the tendency is to close your office door and don't talk to anybody because if you talk with someone, they can ask questions that you don't know the answers to.*
>
> *But that's actually the wrong thing to do, you have to get out there. You have to talk with people and even more important you have to force your management to get out and talk, talk to people, tell them when you don't know but also tell them all the things you know and be a good friend to give people some hope that*

things will get better soon."

In these sessions with the managers, Wim would go over the company's situation honestly and thoroughly, and then they would discuss how to communicate this to the employees. Typical topics of discussion were:

- What can we do as managers?
- What should we say?
- What may employees ask us and how should we answer?
- How should we act?

A key aspect of these meetings was also to listen to the middle managers, so they felt good about the company's situation and could pass that feeling on to their people.

3: Involve employees in decisions

They involved people in all new initiatives by consulting focus groups of employees. They'd get 20 employees together, tell them about what they were planning to do and get their honest feedback.

One specific decision that came out of these focus groups concerned new employees. Originally, the company had planned not to include them in the pay cuts. When this was tested, the new employees protested—they wanted to be treated like everyone else and "share the pain" too.

An intended byproduct of the focus group sessions was that information about the crisis and how it was being handled spread quickly throughout the organization. When the initiatives were announced to the employees, most people had heard about them already, which created more trust.

Wim himself

That was his plan for the organization, but there was another equally important aspect: Wim himself!

On a purely personal level, Wim did three things to handle the crisis. First, he did his best to be positive. Yes, the very survival of the company was at stake, but he still had to believe that there was a way out. Wim put it like this:

"You have to be positive yourself. If you are negative and you come in the factory, everybody's going to be looking at you and getting depressed. So however bad it is, however sad you feel, however worried you are, you come to work in the morning, and you put on a big smile, and you feel optimistic, and you exude optimism and positive thinking.

When you are the CEO, and you see the numbers go down every week or every day, it's very easy to become depressed yourself, and you really have to find the inner strength."

Secondly, he saw the crisis not only as a threat but also as an opportunity to get creative and try something new. To him, creativity and innovation shouldn't just be applied to creating new and exciting products but also to leadership—to find new and exciting solutions to tough problems.

And thirdly, Wim saw this as a chance to prove that there is indeed a better way to handle a crisis than the tried-and-stale ones. He wanted to show the world that this can be handled differently. "I'm gonna show them" may not be the noblest motivation, but it's not uncommon. All the leaders I interviewed for this book expressed the same desire to "show them!"

Now make no mistake, Wim faced a lot of resistance to his approach. He had heated discussions with some board members, who wanted to know why he didn't just lay off 10% of the employees when everyone else in the industry was doing it. The same arguments came from outside the organization from financial analysts, who also would have been much more comfortable with the traditional approach.

Time proved Wim right, and the result of this creative approach to crisis leadership was amazing:

- He kept Xilinx profitable—Except for the second quarter of 2001, when there was an inventory write-down, Xilinx was profitable every quarter of that recession.
- High customer satisfaction—Xilinx kept the same people in sales, so the customers saw the same people they were

used to talking to.

- Increased market share—Xilinx gained 15 points of market share during the crisis. Because they kept their people, they could keep momentum.
- New product development—They had time and people to keep developing new products, which is a huge competitive advantage in their high-tech industry.
- Recruitment and training savings—After three quarters, the market started to improve. Because Xilinx had kept their people, they did not have to spend a ton of money hiring and training new people.
- Motivation and happiness at work—This showed employees that they were truly valued. Not just on paper and in good times, but also in a crisis.

At first, the employees were skeptical, seeing it as a cheap trick. "Yeah, you say you're not doing layoffs, but it's just a matter of time," was a common attitude. But as many other companies in the area had mass layoffs and Xilinx employees saw friends losing their jobs and having to sell their houses, they started to come around. During that time, Xilinx participated in the Fortune Magazine 100 best places to work and came in the top 10—in the middle of the company's worst crisis ever.

The effect was also felt outside the company. One day, about two years after the crisis when Xilinx was back on track, Wim was just arriving at the office when he was approached by a female employee who happened to arrive at the same time. She told him this story:

> *"My husband got laid off, and so yesterday evening we had a family meeting with the children. We had to tell them that their father had been laid off and that they had to do some savings and we had to be very careful how we spend money to make sure that we get through this tough time until our dad finds a job again."*
>
> *One of my children asked 'But, mom, what is going to*

happen if you get laid off?' And I was so proud to say that I work at Xilinx and Xilinx doesn't lay off people."

Wim told me that this was his proudest moment in the whole process.

Being a happy leader is, of course, easiest in good times, when the company is profitable and growing and the results are good. But every company will face a crisis sooner or later. When we look at the incredible success of companies like Apple and IBM today, it's easy to forget that they have both been near bankruptcy not too long ago.

An organization can face tough times due to an economic downturn or failing results, but it can also be due to rapid growth from things going well, from large-scale change projects, changes in leadership, or similar. Happy leaders stick to their principles not only in easy times but also in tough times because they know three things:

1. Most of what companies traditionally do in a crisis doesn't work. The way many organizations typically handle crises is by cutting back on all expenses and doing mass layoffs. While this is sometimes unavoidable, studies actually show that companies who choose this approach recover more slowly[97].
2. It is possible to be happy at work even in a workplace that is in serious trouble. Of course, it's easier to be happy when everything is going swimmingly, but people can still be happy at work in a crisis. It takes determination and focus, but it can be done. Surprisingly, a crisis can make people happy at work, provided that it becomes a reason for people to focus and pull together—rather than an excuse to give up.
3. Happy workplaces get out of a crisis faster. Especially in a crisis, an organization needs to get the best out of its people—and when we're happy at work, we are more motivated, creative, and productive.

More than anything, this requires tremendous personal resources from happy leaders. When the organization is under pressure, it is so easy to fall back on the old ways. Alfred

Josefsen was the CEO of a chain of high-end supermarkets in Denmark called Irma and was known for making it a very happy workplace. When the financial crisis hit Denmark in 2008, he saw an immediate drop in revenue across all stores and was facing tremendous pressure from analysts, pundits, and fellow CEOs to do what everyone else was doing and start introducing layoffs and cutting costs. I interviewed him about it, and this was his reaction:

> *Hell no, that's just too primitive. A monkey could do that. Instead, I told our leadership team that our model has been so successful in good times, now it's time to show that it works in tough times. This is the time for us to show that we're serious when we say that employees come first.*

It worked. Irma avoided layoffs and kept growing and achieving record profits under Alfred's leadership. When times are tough, leaders may face tremendous pressure to give up their values and "do what needs to be done." Bob Sutton, author of the excellent book "Good Boss, Bad Boss" tells this story from the very early days at Pixar:

> Pixar was under financial pressure, and much of this pressure came down on the heads of the Division's leaders, Ed Catmull and Alvy Ray Smith.
>
> The new president, Doug Norby, wanted to bring some discipline to Lucasfilm and was pressing Catmull and Smith to do some fairly deep layoffs. The two couldn't bring themselves to do it.
>
> But Norby was unmoved. He was pestering Ed and Alvy for a list of names from the Computer Division to lay off, and Ed and Alvy kept blowing him off. Finally came the order: "You will be in my office tomorrow morning at 9:00 with a list of names."
>
> So what did these two bosses do? They showed up in his office at 9:00 and plunked down a list. It had two names on it: Ed Catmull and Alvy Ray Smith.

You can't always avoid layoffs, but if you believe in leading with happiness, you must live by it in good times and bad. Here is one of my favorite examples from Rosenbluth International:

> A company's commitment to its values is most thoroughly tested in adversity, and Rosenbluth hit its share of adversity right after 9/11. Overnight, corporate travel was reduced to a fraction of its former level, and it recovered more slowly than anyone predicted.
>
> Rosenbluth tried everything in their power to avoid layoffs. They cut expenses. Staff took pay cuts and so did managers and executives. But in the end they had to face it: Layoffs were inevitable, and they decided to fire 1,000 of their 6,000 employees. It was either that or close the whole company in six months. How do you handle this situation in a company that puts its people first?
>
> In his book's most moving chapter, an epilogue written after 9/11, Hal Rosenbluth explains that though layoffs don't make employees happy, not doing the layoffs and then going bankrupt at a later date would have made even more people even more unhappy.
>
> Hal Rosenbluth recounts how he wrote a letter to the organization explaining the decision and the thinking behind it in detail. The result was amazing: People who'd been fired streamed into Hal's office, many in tears, telling him they understood and thanking him for their time at the company.
>
> Rosenbluth's letter also contained a pledge: That those remaining at the company would do everything they could to bring the company back on track so they could rehire those who'd lost their jobs. Six months later, they'd hired back 500 out of the 1,000, and the company was solidly on its way to recovery.

Leading with happiness is not about avoiding the tough decisions—it's about making them in a way that is consistent with your values. Especially in hard times.

If you have their backs, they'll have yours

> Market Basket is a chain of 78 Supermarkets with 25,000 employees across New England. Their biggest crisis came in 2014, not because of financial hard times but due to an internal power struggle between two cousins, Arthur T.

Demoulas, the CEO, and Arthur S. Demoulas, who also owned a significant amount of stock and was on the board of directors[98]. The names are confusing, but the story is great.

Arthur T. had been the CEO since 2008 during which time the company grew from 14,000 employees to 25,000. He was loved by his employees and was known for his ability to remember their names, birthdays, and milestones, attending many of their weddings and funerals, checking in on ill employees, and asking about the spouses and children of his workers.

In 2014, Arthur S. managed to gain a majority on the board of directors and fire Arthur T. The new leadership signaled that employees had been treated much too generously until now and should expect less beneficial working conditions. On the other hand, the board also voted to distribute $250 million to family shareholders, an action opposed by Arthur T.

This could have been a sad story of yet another company with a great culture ruined by a change in top management, but the employees of Market Basket did not simply take this lying down. They instituted a series of protests and rallies in front of the stores and the HQ, refused to stock the stores so shelves were empty, and sales came to a halt and even enlisted customers to the fight. They resisted all threats of firings and reprisals from the board and also kept them from bringing in new employees.

Eventually, the board caved, and they ended up selling the company to Arthur T. and a group of investors. He celebrated his triumphant return with an emotional speech at a big rally of Market Basket employees, which included the words[99]:

"It's great to be back together with you.

Words cannot express how much I appreciate each and every one of you.

Words cannot express how much I missed you and words cannot express how much I love you."

In an incredible effort, employees and suppliers managed to

restock shelves in all the supermarkets in a matter of hours and days, and business was quickly booming again and has only grown ever since.

All leaders want their employees to be engaged and genuinely care about the welfare of the business, but happy leaders recognize that this engagement has to go both ways. People will go through fire for happy leaders, as this story shows. If you genuinely care about your people, they will care right back and do the extraordinary for you.

This chapter in tweets

- If you have your employees' backs in good times, they will have yours in bad times.
- In tough times you need every employee to perform at their best. They can only do that if they're happy at work.
- If you want employees to care about the company, the company has to care about them.
- Any idiot can do staff layoffs in a crisis. Good leaders look for a better way.
- Staying happy in tough times is hard but more necessary than ever.

The challenges of leading with happiness

"It's cold at the top."

"If my employees are happy, they're not working hard enough."

"It's a dog-eat-dog world in business."

"Nice guys finish last."

If you listen to traditional wisdom about leadership, you would never suspect that it has anything to do with happiness. The traditional views of business and leadership are much more about competition, ambition, and power.

So if happiness is that fantastic, why don't all leaders focus on it? Why is the world of business still influenced by a very different worldview? What challenges might you face as a happy leader?

There are some powerful forces pulling us in a completely different direction, systematically teaching leaders very different mindsets and creating advantages for a very different kind of leader. In this chapter, we'll look at some of those forces and how to counter them.

Business schools are stuck in the past

Bob Chapman, the CEO and chairman of Barry-Wehmiller, has chosen to lead in a way that values every single one of his 12,000 employees. But this is not how he was educated. He describes his formal business education like this[100]:

> *Unfortunately, we live in a world of capitalism where we see people as objects for our success. I was educated and raised in an environment where creating shareholder value and profits would result in my success. I took management classes, I got a management degree, I got a job in management so what did I try and do: I tried to manage people.*
>
> *I was never taught the awesome responsibility that leadership has over the lives that are influenced by my leadership. I was raised and educated that capitalism was about profits, shareholder value, and my success.*
>
> *I think from this perspective that we have a crisis in this country. A crisis of leadership and many of the symptoms we are seeing with broken families, broken marriages, and broken lives are the result of us sending people home each day with a sense that they work for an organization that doesn't care about them.*
>
> *The good news is that we have the power to solve this tomorrow. We just need to engage our heads and our hearts in a leadership process that validates the worth of every individual.*

In order to be a good leader, Chapman had to actively unlearn much of what he'd been taught in business school.

My latest addiction is the website Coursera, which offers thousands of online university-level classes free of charge. I have followed fascinating courses in everything from neuroeconomics to osteoarcheology. It's a wonderful way to spend an hour or two in the evening, since it's not only entertaining but will also teach you many new things about the world.

In 2015, I thought I would check out some of their more business-oriented offerings, so I signed up for several, including one called "Foundations of Business Strategy" offered by the University of Virginia. And let me tell you, where most Coursera courses inspire me and expand my horizons, this one just left me unspeakably depressed.

The entire focus of the course was to analyze any given market in order to increase profits for a firm. There was zero mention of topics like culture, employee wellbeing, CSR, or sustainability. Not only was there no sense that any of those things *should* matter, the course actively went out of its way to ignore them.

At one point, the professor mentioned Southwest Airlines as a case, and I sat up straight and thought "Finally, here it comes." Southwest is, of course, famous for saying that their main competitive advantage is their employees and making this their top strategic priority, but this course *never mentioned that at all.*

Let me hammer this point home: The course examined one of the world's most profitable airlines, where top executives *clearly say themselves* that their success is mainly due to their strategic focus on making employees and customers happy, but then never mentioned any of that and instead chose to focus only on market forces.

If this is what business schools teach people, it's no wonder that their graduates come out into the world holding traditional views skewed entirely towards profits and results. The problem is that business school graduates dominate in leadership. In many workplaces, you will not be considered for management positions over a certain level if you don't have a business degree of some kind.

In addition to business schools, many larger organizations have their own internal leadership academies, and I think it's safe to say that not many of those have put happiness on the curriculum yet.

Of course, not all business schools are like that. I recently met with Lena Rübelmann and Juliana Wolfsberger, two students from the School of Economics and Management at

Lund University in Sweden, who wanted to interview me for their thesis project on the 30-hour work week.

It turned out that these students had come from two big business schools in Germany and Austria and had chosen to break away from the thinking of these institutions precisely because they were too focused on an outdated and profit-driven view of leadership and business. In Lund, they found a program that gets it, offering a modern, science-based business curriculum that fully acknowledges the role of happiness and long-term thinking in business. We need more of those business schools and fewer of the traditional ones.

Happy leaders are sometimes weeded out

> Lisa was promoted to team leader of a call center team in the UK after working in that team for two years. As an employee, she'd noticed many problems that she immediately went about addressing, constantly involving her team of 17 people in defining what kind of culture and working style suited them best. The results were positive—her team became more engaged and the results improved vastly.
>
> After six months, she was pulled aside by her leader and told that her leadership style had been noticed and that she would have to change if she wanted to stay on as manager.
>
> "You're much too chummy with your employees. What if you have to fire one of them? You'll have to create much more respect around yourself as a leader."
>
> Lisa was shocked and disheartened that everything she'd done to create a happy team, and which had also resulted in much better results, was not only being ignored by higher-ups but was actively discouraged. She refused to change and while she has remained as manager of that team and results are consistently great, she has received no recognition for it and has not been encouraged to seek further promotion.
>
> Meanwhile, other team leaders whose teams are not only miserable but also less productive have been given accolades and promotions ahead of her.

Given that traditional thinking in business is most decidedly *not* about happiness, it's no wonder that leadership selection and promotion in many workplaces either does not value happiness at all or, in some cases, has a direct anti-happiness bias.

In one study, volunteers were asked to read a speech and rate the intelligence of the person who wrote it. Half the volunteers read a speech that was against the topic, the other half read the same speech but with a few words changed so the author was now for the topic. The participants rated the negative person who was against the speech as more intelligent on average. This shows a common bias against happy, positive people, seeing them as less competent, less intelligent, less serious, and more naive.

Some societies have this to a larger degree. For instance, the French author Flaubert once wrote:

> *To be stupid, selfish, and have good health are three requirements for happiness, though if stupidity is lacking, all is lost.*

This perception is of course completely wrong. I hope I've been able to demonstrate to you that happy people indeed have better functioning minds, more cognitive resources and are more likely to succeed in anything they do.

Unhappy leaders promote in their own image

We tend to promote in our own image. When a results-driven, hard-nosed, competitive CEO is looking for a new VP, there is every chance that he will promote or hire someone who is also results-driven, hard-nosed, and competitive. And then the cycle repeats itself when that VP goes looking for a new department head.

The company may have very pretty things written on their website about how "people are our most important asset." They may have inspiring values like *respect* and *integrity*. But if they keep promoting people leaders with a results-only mindset, none of it will ever be more than pretty words.

This can be a true disaster when the company has a jerk at

the top. When Stanford professor Bob Sutton started to write a book about the hidden costs of jerks at work, he wanted to go full monty and call the book "The No Asshole Rule." Gasp! Yes! The A-word. He wasn't writing about jerks or bullies—he was writing about flaming assholes and what they cost people and businesses.

His first choice of publisher, The Harvard Business School Press, was happy to publish the book if he would change the title to something less offensive. So, he was forced to change... publishers.

In the book, Sutton convincingly demonstrates using surveys, psychological studies, and case stories that workplace jerks are far more trouble than they're worth. They may be getting results and making the numbers, but they do so at a huge cost to the rest of the organization and to the well-being of the people around them.

Just to make it worse, assholes *breed*. No, not with each other (a horrible thought in itself!). Not only do jerks tend to bring out the worst in others (creating more jerks), they also tend to hire and promote jerks like themselves, or they make sure to hire people who are too weak to oppose them.

In order to combat this, many companies have introduced a "No asshole rule"—though they may call it something else out of politeness. Quirk, a social media agency in Cape Town, South Africa was forced to introduce a similar rule after they hired a VP who turned out to be a complete jerk and who ended up causing enormous harm to both employee and customer relations.

They never wanted to risk that happening again, so they added a new ingenious hiring practice called "The Christmas Party Test." After a number of job interviews, the prospective new manager goes out for coffee with the team she will lead. There is no discussion of work or professional skills—this is purely social. On returning to the office, every employee must answer one question: "Do I want to sit next to this person at our next company Christmas Party?" If one employee says no, they don't hire that person.

Dan Jacobs of Apple put it most simply:

It's better to have a hole in your team than an asshole in your team.

"Work sucks—everybody knows that."

The Drew Carey show is a classic 90s sitcom that follows a lovable group of losers in Cleveland, Ohio. In my favorite scene, Drew is talking to his co-worker Kate, both of whom are miserable in their jobs at the fictional department store Winfred-Louder. Here is their exchange:

> Kate: "I hate my job."
>
> Drew: "You hate your job? Well, why didn't you say so. You know, there's a support group for that. It's called EVERYBODY. They meet at the bar."

I've always wondered why so many people put up with bad jobs and bad bosses. Why are many people desperately unhappy with their manager (up to 50% according to some studies) but accept this as normal?

Here's why: We're carrying massive cultural baggage. Through much of Western history, there has been a sense that work is hard and unpleasant and that's why we get paid to do it.

This is expressed most clearly in Max Weber's biblically-based work "The Protestant Work Ethic," which was used by Protestant preachers to preach that hard labor was good for people, good for Christian society, and a salve for original sin. According to Christianity, humans used to live in the Garden of Eden, where everything was perfect. But because of original sin we were ejected and, according to Genesis 3:19, this is our situation now:

> *"By the sweat of your brow you will eat your food until you return to the ground, since from it you were taken; for dust you are and to dust you will return."*

According to the Hebrew belief, work is a "curse devised by God explicitly to punish the disobedience and ingratitude of Adam and Eve." The Old Testament itself supports work, not because there's any joy in it, but because it is necessary to prevent poverty and destitution.

The ancient Greek word for work is ponos, which means sorrow. According to Plato, manual labor was for slaves, while free men were supposed to pursue warfare, commerce, and the arts, especially architecture or sculpture[101].

So, according to western cultural roots, work is a curse, a punishment for original sin, and only for slaves. In short, work is hell, and we must endure it because we're all sinners, but don't worry, we'll get our reward once we're dead! Any questions?

So, if the way a leader leads is causing misery, stress, and frustration, many people will just accept that as normal. It may never have occurred to them that it could ever be different.

In our quest for happy leadership, we are going up against thoughts and beliefs that have been deeply embedded in our culture for millennia. This is why we need a conscious leadership revolution in workplaces all around the world and why those of us who have chosen to break away from the old attitude to work need to support each other.

No pain, no gain

Have you seen the movie Whiplash? If not, watch it first chance you get! It is not only a great movie but also the perfect example of the "success through suffering" narrative that permeates the business world. In the movie, a young jazz drumming prodigy is tortured relentlessly by his sadistic teacher, and the extreme mental and physical pain he suffers makes him a great drummer.

There are numerous other movies and books that subscribe to the same basic worldview, according to which you can only achieve success through sacrifice and pain and the more it hurts, the more successful you will ultimately be.

In popular culture, the only stories where someone achieves success through happiness, are stories like "Forrest Gump" and "Big" where fools or children achieve success through their innocence and naiveté. This just serves to strengthen the narrative that only the dumb and the hapless achieve success through happiness. This worldview is common, but false. There is much more success to be found (in business, in art, and in life) in fun, happiness, camaraderie, and in simply enjoying what you do on the whole.

In real life, there are many examples. Richard Branson clearly attributes his success to the fact that he's enjoyed himself along the way. Ben and Jerry, the ice cream makers, say the same thing and so does Yvon Chouinard of Patagonia, Herb Kelleher of Southwest Airlines, Tony Hsieh of Zappos, and many others.

I find it telling that, Damien Chazelle, the director of Whiplash was a serious drumming student as a young man and has this to say about that time:

> [I was in] a very competitive jazz band that was modeled after professional bands. And I remember being very terrified. That was my overall emotion during those years. Just dread. And not being able to eat meals before rehearsals and losing sleep and sweating my ass off.

To this day, he still gets nauseated when he sees a drum kit so when it came time to do the movie, here's how he wanted to do it:

> I like a set to be a happy place, where people can feel free to experiment. Especially, for instance, with this set. We only had 20 days to shoot the whole movie. The stress and the anxiety were just inherent in the schedule. So I tried to make it as stress-free of a set as possible.

The whole "success through suffering" mindset is not only wrong, I think it's become so pervasive that it's become self-reinforcing. Leaders expect work to be tough, expect to have to sacrifice many other aspects of their lives to "make it"—and if that's what you expect, then there's a good chance that's how it will end up.

Leaders with this mindset also look at happy employees and teams with mistrust. They may not directly mind that they are happy, but they harbor a sneaking suspicion that since success comes from suffering, these happy employees could get even better results if only they were working harder and less happily. They may then exert direct or indirect pressures to make people work more in a way that fits their perceptions better.

Also, once leaders do become successful and start analyzing

what worked for them, this narrative means that they're more likely to attribute their success to all the "hard work" and their sacrifices—even though their success may just as well have come from the times they had fun, the help they got from people who liked them, or a supportive environment they found themselves in.

The very idea that you, as a leader, can slave away in stress and fear and frustration for years and sacrifice everything else in your life and THEN achieve your goals and just turn around and be happy seems very suspect to me. If you've been in pain for that long, that pain is most likely going to stay with you, and you will be successful and unhappy.

Power does bad things to us

It turns out that having power over others can lead to some quite negative behaviors. One simple but fascinating experiment from Berkeley University is called the "cookie monster" experiment. Researchers placed college students in groups of three and gave them an assignment to collaborate on a short policy paper on a social issue. They then randomly told one of the students that he would evaluate the performance of the other two after they finished the task. If he gave them good ratings, they could earn points that would increase their chance to win a cash bonus. That person now had a little more power over the other two.

After they had been working for a while, the researchers casually brought the three subjects a plate with *four* cookies. They found that not only did the disinhibited "powerful" students eat more than their share of the cookies, but they were also more likely to chew with their mouths open and to scatter crumbs over the table! It seems that whenever we are given power, we become a little more focused on ourselves and a little less focused on others if we're not careful.

A similar study from the same researchers made people play games of Monopoly that were heavily rigged in the favor of one player who started with twice as much money, got two dice instead of one, and got more money for passing 'go'. Basically, there was no way that player could not end up winning the game.

As in the cookie monster study, that person became ruder, louder, and ate more (and more messily) from the bowl of pretzels set out for the players. But the scariest finding came from the interviews they did with the winning players after the game. You'd think that they would just admit that the game was clearly rigged in their favor, and that's why they won—but instead, they tended to explain their victory more in terms of their own strategies and skills.

If we combine the results of several of these studies, we see that having power and privilege can make leaders:

- Less ethical and more likely to lie or cheat.
- Less prosocial and more selfish.
- Less generous.
- Less empathetic.
- More likely to flirt inappropriately.
- More prone to risky behavior.
- More likely to explain their success in terms of their own actions/skills rather than any privilege they were given.
- Less likely to value the contributions of others.

It's easy to see how these effects can combine to cause harmful behavior in leaders.

The good news

The forces mentioned here are strong, but they are not all-powerful. While they generally influence leaders to engage in behaviors that undermine happiness, they can be countered and overcome.

And fortunately, more and more leaders realize that this is necessary. A 2014 survey of 300,000 leaders and employees asked what competencies were most important for leaders. The most popular reply was "Inspire and motivate others."[102]

There are two ways leaders can avoid falling for these forces:

1. Get educated. Leaders who know about these forces are more likely to resist their effects. So, simply by telling you about them, I've now made you less likely to fall prey

to them. You're welcome!
2. Find peers who share your beliefs. It's much easier to stick to your guns and do what you know is right when you have people around you who share your beliefs.

This chapter in tweets

- Traditional views of leadership are not about happiness but about competition, status, and power. We must change that.
- Most business schools and leadership training ignores the value of happiness and focus solely on profits. Which, ironically, hurts profits.
- Some cultures and organizations are actively anti-happiness, calling it silly, naïve, or frivolous. Don't fall for it.
- Bad leaders promote in their own image, spreading more misery.
- Thousands of years of history tells us that work, by definition, sucks. It's time to change that.
- "No pain, no gain" is the battle cry of bad leaders everywhere. It's plain wrong—happiness leads to better results than suffering.
- Power makes us more likely to lie or cheat, more selfish, and less likely to value others' contributions. Leaders must know and resist this.

Go forth and be happy

> *The most dangerous leadership myth is that leaders are born—that there is a genetic factor to leadership. This myth asserts that people simply either have certain charismatic qualities or not.*
>
> *That's nonsense; in fact, the opposite is true. Leaders are made rather than born.*
>
> *–Warren Bennis*

I hope this book has clearly demonstrated that there should be more to leadership and business than the ruthless pursuit of a company's financial goals and the leader's career ambitions in a way that completely ignores the well-being of people and the planet. Indeed, this type of leadership is not only distasteful, it is ethically wrong.

If you've felt that way, then you are definitely not alone. Leaders at all levels, all over the world from many different domains agree and have dedicated their leadership to making the world better and happier.

This is not easy, and you will have to go against traditional business thinking. As Bob Chapman told me, "It takes courage to care in the business environment we live in today. It's much easier to simply rely on profitability, cash generation, shareholder value."

I have three tips for you that may help. My number one tip is to do *something*. While this book has hopefully offered you many suggestions and ideas for things you might do, none of them work unless you do them. In doing this, you're going to occasionally get it wrong, and that's OK. Leadership is not an exact science, and even the best of intentions do not guarantee perfect action. This is where it's important to remember the words of Theodore Roosevelt:

> *It is not the critic who counts; not the man who points out how the strong man stumbles, or where the doer of deeds could have done them better.*
>
> *The credit belongs to the man who is actually in the arena, whose face is marred by dust and sweat and blood; who strives valiantly; who errs, who comes short again and again, because there is no effort without error and shortcoming; but who does actually strive to do the deeds; who knows great enthusiasms, the great devotions; who spends himself in a worthy cause; who at the best knows in the end the triumph of high achievement, and who at the worst, if he fails, at least fails while daring greatly, so that his place shall never be with those cold and timid souls who neither know victory nor defeat.*

My second tip is to find accomplices and like-minded people. It's hard to go against prevailing business wisdom alone, no matter how wrong and boneheaded that "wisdom" may be. If you can find a small group of people who share your belief that leadership is all about creating a better and happier world, it will be much easier to sustain your progress.

And my final tip is to celebrate your wins. When you get it right, when you come up with a clever idea that works, or when you can see that you're having the effect you want on yourself and others, don't keep it to yourself—celebrate it loudly and proudly. That way you can maintain your own sense of progress and even inspire others on their journey.

At this book's accompanying website, you will find many additional resources and recommended readings, and you can also download a free workbook with five great exercises to get you started, including these:

- Write your career obituary
- Define what kind of leader you want to be
- Make your business case for happiness

Have a look at www.leadingwithhappiness.com.

And remember: Research clearly shows that happy people are more creative, productive, and motivated. They are smarter and learn faster. They care more about others, and consequentially others care more about them. They communicate better and have an easier time recruiting people for their cause.

And that is why the future doesn't belong to the rich. The future doesn't belong to the powerful. And the future doesn't belong to the ruthless.

The future belongs to the happy.

Links and references

1 Milton Friedman, "The business of business is business": http://www.nytimes.com/1970/09/13/archives/a-friedman-doctrine-the-social-responsibility-of-business-is-to.html

2 Epicurus on friendship: https://plato.stanford.edu/entries/epicurus/

3 Epicurus on virtue as a path to happiness: http://classics.mit.edu/Epicurus/princdoc.html

4 Epicurus on why you shouldn't fear death: http://classics.mit.edu/Epicurus/menoec.html

5 Epicurus accused of orgies: https://fee.org/articles/what-epicurus-can-teach-us-about-freedom-and-happiness/

6 Løgstrup's ethical demand: https://en.wikipedia.org/wiki/Knud_Ejler_L%C3%B8gstrup#The_Ethical_Demand

7 A scary example of conformity—Asch's conformity experiment: https://www.youtube.com/watch?v=TYIh4MkcfJA

8 An even scarier example of how a toxic culture creates toxic behavior—The Stanford Prison Experiment: https://www.youtube.com/watch?v=sZwfNs1pqG0

9 The Milgram Experiment: https://nature.berkeley.edu/ucce50/ag-labor/7article/article35.htm

10 IKEA's company vision: http://www.ikea.com/ms/en_SG/about_ikea/our_business_idea/index.html

11 Positive psychology: https://ppc.sas.upenn.edu/

12 Nearly half of happiness can be accounted for by genetic factors: https://mctfr.psych.umn.edu/research/happiness.html

13 You can raise your long-term happiness over time: http://sonjalyubomirsky.com/wp-content/themes/sonjalyubomirsky/papers/LSS2005.pdf

14 Happy people experience frequent positive emotions: https://www.ncbi.nlm.nih.gov/pmc/articles/PMC3126102/

15 Barbara Fredrickson's Broaden and Build Theory: https://www.ncbi.nlm.nih.gov/pmc/articles/PMC3122271/

16 Positive emotions make us more creative: https://hbr.org/2011/05/the-power-of-small-wins

17 Positive emotions cause better health: http://www.tandfonline.com/doi/abs/10.1080/17437190701492486

18 In aging twins, the happier twin lives longer: https://www.ncbi.nlm.nih.gov/pmc/articles/PMC3105329/

Links and references

[19] How emotional states affect people: https://www.ncbi.nlm.nih.gov/pubmed/16351326

[20] Satisfaction has fewer beneficial effects than positive emotions: https://www.princeton.edu/~kahneman/docs/Publications/Living_DK_JR_2005.pdf

[21] Measuring happiness: https://internal.psychology.illinois.edu/~ediener/scales.html

[22] Emotional contagion in meetings: http://web.media.mit.edu/~tod/media/pdfs/EmotionalContagion.pdf

[23] Negativity bias—bad is stronger than good http://assets.csom.umn.edu/assets/71516.pdf

[24] The brain is like velcro for negative experiences: https://www.ncbi.nlm.nih.gov/pubmed/15701224

[25] Gratitude makes us happier: http://www.health.harvard.edu/newsletter_article/in-praise-of-gratitude

[26] Berkeley's Great Good in Action Center: https://ggia.berkeley.edu/

[27] The Grant Longitudinal Study: https://www.theatlantic.com/magazine/archive/2013/05/thanks-mom/309287/

[28] Warm relationships matter more than IQ for lifetime income: https://www.amazon.com/Triumphs-Experience-Harvard-Grant-Study/dp/0674059824

[29] Helping behavior in toddlers: https://www.ncbi.nlm.nih.gov/pmc/articles/PMC3088085/

[30] Devastatingly cute video of helping toddlers: https://www.youtube.com/watch?v=aS-QLB8ELyk

[31] Neuroscience enhances our understanding of happiness: https://www.ncbi.nlm.nih.gov/pmc/articles/PMC3008658/

[32] Mirror neurons: http://www.apa.org/monitor/oct05/mirror.aspx

[33] Social isolation lights up the brain the same way as physical pain: https://www.ncbi.nlm.nih.gov/pubmed/22286852

[34] Happiness is intensely social: https://greatergood.berkeley.edu/article/item/the_neuroscience_of_happiness

[35] Our brains are hardwired to do the right thing: https://www.ncbi.nlm.nih.gov/pmc/articles/PMC3163302/

Links and references

[36] Men derive pleasure from seeing cheaters punished: https://www.newscientist.com/article/dn8605-brain-scans-reveal-mens-pleasure-in-revenge/

[37] Herb Kelleher—"What drives me is to do right by other people and to serve them with excellence": https://youtu.be/wxyC3Ywb9yc?t=24m

[38] Faking happiness at work makes people less happy and more stressed: https://www.ncbi.nlm.nih.gov/pmc/articles/PMC1420709/

[39] Positive thinking doesn't work: https://hbr.org/2014/10/stop-being-so-positive

[40] Managers' moods directly impact employees: twincities.bizjournals.com/twincities/stories/2006/02/20/daily30.html

[41] Unhappy workers are less happy in life: http://www.tandfonline.com/doi/abs/10.1207/s15324834basp0101_4

[42] Unhappy workers gain weight: http://www.ncbi.nlm.nih.gov/pubmed/24351544

[43] Unhappiness at work harms relationships: http://metro.co.uk/2012/04/10/womens-sex-lives-ruined-by-job-stress-claims-new-study-382318/

[44] Unhappy workers have higher risk of depression: http://onlinelibrary.wiley.com/doi/10.1348/096317909X478557/abstract

[45] Unhappy workers have higher risk of heart attacks: https://www.ncbi.nlm.nih.gov/pubmed/26238744

[46] Unhappy workers have higher risk of strokes: https://www.webmd.com/stroke/news/20151014/job-stress-tied-to-stroke-risk-study-suggests

[47] Unhappy workers more at risk for cancer: http://news.bbc.co.uk/2/hi/health/763401.stm

[48] Bosses are generally happier than employees: http://www.pewsocialtrends.org/2014/01/09/why-its-great-to-be-the-boss/

[49] Bosses have more autonomy, control and opportunities to learn: http://publications.jrc.ec.europa.eu/repository/bitstream/JRC59720/reqno_jrc59720_managers_happier_eur_report_final.pdf%5B1%5D.pdf

[50] Sitting down all day is bad for you: https://opinionator.blogs.nytimes.com/2010/02/23/stand-up-while-you-read-this/

[51] Physical activity improves job performance: https://hbr.org/2014/10/regular-exercise-is-part-of-your-job

Links and references

[52] Find a form of exercise you enjoy: https://link.springer.com/article/10.1007%2Fs11002-014-9301-6

[53] "I prioritize sleep": http://www.huffingtonpost.com/2015/02/17/importance-of-sleep_n_6697650.html

[54] Sleep deprivation carries tremendous costs: https://www.ncbi.nlm.nih.gov/pmc/articles/PMC3564638/

[55] Leaders who sleep badly mistreat employees: https://hbr.org/2014/11/research-your-abusive-boss-is-probably-an-insomniac

[56] Sleep classes at Next Jump: http://www.huffingtonpost.com/charlie-kim/sleep-is-a-companys-probl_b_9668834.html

[57] Introverts are happier when they're in the company of other people: https://www.psychologytoday.com/blog/web-loneliness/201406/yes-its-true-introverts-are-less-happy-extroverts

[58] The best thing a manager can do to prevent work stress is to develop good relationships with the employees at work: https://www.bi.edu/research/business-review/articles/2014/08/less-stress-when-work-relationships-are-good/

[59] The benefits of keeping a work journal: https://hbr.org/2007/05/inner-work-life-understanding-the-subtext-of-business-performance

[60] The benefits of keeping a work journal: https://hbr.org/2011/04/four-reasons-to-keep-a-work-di

[61] Negative cognitive effects of time scarcity: http://www.apa.org/monitor/2014/02/scarcity.aspx

[62] In praise of slack: Time is of the essence: https://www.jstor.org/stable/4165766?seq=1#page_scan_tab_contents

[63] CNN article with terrible advice from famous leaders on how to kill yourself with overwork: http://money.cnn.com/2006/03/02/news/newsmakers/howiwork_fortune_032006/index.htm

[64] Leaders are available 72 hours a week on average: http://www.ccl.org/leadership/pdf/research/AlwaysOn.pdf

[65] Working 55 hours a week increases risk of stroke by 33%: http://www.theguardian.com/lifeandstyle/2015/aug/20/working-longer-hours-increases-stroke-risk

[66] Overwork doesn't result in higher output: https://hbr.org/2015/08/the-research-is-clear-long-hours-backfire-for-people-and-for-companies

[67] Herb Kelleher: Employees are job one: https://youtu.be/wxyC3Ywb9yc?t=27m

Links and references

[68] People with bad workplace relationships had a 240% increased risk of dying from heart disease: https://www.ncbi.nlm.nih.gov/pubmed/21553970

[69] Southwest Airlines choose managers with great relationship skills: Systemic Change Management: The Five Capabilities for Improving Enterprises By G. Roth, A. DiBella

[70] Happy employees lead to higher customer loyalty, sales and growth: https://hbr.org/2008/07/putting-the-service-profit-chain-to-work

[71] A positive environment will lead to dramatic benefits for employers, employees, and the bottom line: https://hbr.org/2015/12/proof-that-positive-work-cultures-are-more-productive

[72] Positive feedback makes us happier, less stressed, and more productive: https://papers.ssrn.com/sol3/papers.cfm?abstract_id=2662057

[73] Study of unhappiness at work: https://woohooinc.com/happiness-at-work/study-bad-work-days-how-common-are-they-and-what-makes-them-bad/

[74] Recognition builds identity and relationships: https://plato.stanford.edu/entries/recognition/

[75] Valve's employee handbook: http://www.valvesoftware.com/company/Valve_Handbook_LowRes.pdf

[76] Ajax football talent spotter looks for kids who love the game: http://www.nytimes.com/2010/06/06/magazine/06Soccer-t.html

[77] Consequences of bullying: https://www.ncbi.nlm.nih.gov/pmc/articles/PMC4382139/

[78] Non-Violent Communication: http://www.nonviolentcommunication.com/

[79] Ben and Jerry's flavor graveyard: http://www.benjerry.com/flavors/flavor-graveyard

[80] Happy employees make customers happier through emotional contagion: http://bear.warrington.ufl.edu/weitz/mar7786/Articles/Hennig-Thurau %202006%20emotional%20labor.pdf

[81] WD-40 highlights users' best tips: https://wd40.com/uses-tips

[82] Innocent Drink's Big Knit: http://www.thebigknit.co.uk/

[83] Meet the knitter: http://www.thebigknit.co.uk/meet-the-knitters

[84] Southwest Airlines employee regularly breaks out his ukulele: https://southwest.fm/southwest-music-scene/a-man-and-a-ukulele/

[85] No scripts at Zappos: https://hbr.org/2010/07/how-i-did-it-zappos-ceo-on-going-to-extremes-for-customers

Links and references

[86] Craigslist's founder Craig Newmark on his main role being in customer support: https://www.quora.com/Who-made-you-the-person-you-are-today/answer/Craig-Newmark-1

[87] DaVita employee finds "Big Mama" after Katrina: http://www.nxtbook.com/nxtbooks/davita/2007fall/index.php?startid=11#/10

[88] Southwest Airlines holds plane for family of murder victim: http://www.elliott.org/blog/southwest-airlines-pilot-holds-plane-for-murder-victims-family/

[89] Southwest spokesperson on holding a plane for family of a murder victim: http://edition.cnn.com/2011/TRAVEL/01/14/southwest.pilot.holds.flight/index.html

[90] Patagonia ad "Don't Buy This Jacket": https://www.patagonia.com/blog/2011/11/dont-buy-this-jacket-black-friday-and-the-new-york-times/

[91] The B Corp Movement: https://www.bcorporation.net/

[92] Ben and Jerry's on Fairtrade and treating suppliers well: http://www.benjerry.com/values/issues-we-care-about/fairtrade

[93] The legendary Zappos Vendor Party: http://www.zappos.com/about/untamed-circus

[94] Analysts tell Costco to stop treating employees so well: http://www.nytimes.com/2005/07/17/business/yourmoney/17costco.html?ex=1279252800&en=8b31033c5b6a6d68&ei=5088

[95] Shareholders do not own the company: https://www.ft.com/content/7bd1b20a-879b-11e5-90de-f44762bf9896

[96] Southwest Airlines CEO shares moving story at shareholders meeting: https://www.youtube.com/watch?v=VOkwtB5SLVY

[97] Companies who do layoffs in tough times recover more slowly: https://hbr.org/2007/07/layoffs-evidence-on-costs-and

[98] The power struggle at Market Basket: https://en.wikipedia.org/wiki/DeMoulas_Market_Basket

[99] The triumphant speech Demoulas gave to employees after coming back as CEO of Market Basket: https://www.youtube.com/watch?v=-0vYmy7tIPs

[100] Bob Chapman's TEDx Speech on Truly Human Leadership: https://www.youtube.com/watch?v=njn-lIEv1LU

[101] Ancient Greek attitudes towards work: http://workethic.coe.uga.edu/hatcp.html

Links and references

[102] Leaders say most important leadership skill is to inspire and motivate others: https://hbr.org/2014/07/the-skills-leaders-need-at-every-level

26177583R00107

Printed in Great Britain
by Amazon